For Michael Joseph

With best wishes

[signature]
10/21/11

DAM FOOLISHNESS

Raff Ellis

Dam Foolishness
& Other Recollections

A Memoir by Raff Ellis

Cune

Dam Foolishness & Other Recollections
© *2011 Raff Ellis*
Cune Press, Seattle 2011

ISBN 13: 978-1885942227
Hardcover $27.95

Library of Congress Cataloging-in-Publication Data
Ellis, Raff, 1931-
Dam Foolishness & Other Recollections: a memoir as told
through short stories / Raff Ellis.
p. cm.
ISBN-13: 978-1-885942-22-7 (hardcover)
ISBN-10: 1-885942-22-2 (hardcover)
1. Ellis, Raff, 1931- 2. Lebanese Americans--Biography.
3. Ellis, Raff, 1931---Childhood and youth. 4. Carthage
(N.Y.)--Biography. 5. Carthage (N.Y.)--Social life and customs. I. Title.
E184.L34E43 2011
974.7'57--dc22
2010048443

Thanks to Chris Ellis of Entropy Design
for cover illustrations and for the
treatment of interior photos.
All photos are used with permission.
For details see page 238 (Acknowledgements).
For more information contact the author:
raff.ellis@yahoo.com
www.rafellis.com

Cune Press

PO Box 31024, Seattle, WA 98103

www.cunepress.com | www.cunepress.net

To all those, past and present, whose roots permeate small town America, and whose memories live forever.

...Oh you children who go singing
To the Town down the River...
Tell me what you know to-day;
Tell me how far you are going,
Tell me how you find your way.
Oh you children who are dreaming,
Tell me what you dream to-day."

—*The Town Down by The River*
   by Edwin Arlington Robinson

Carthage, NY

Foreword

THE STORIES IN THIS WORK ARE BASED on actual persons, places, and experiences. In many cases the names have been changed to protect both the innocent and the guilty, living and dead.

Anyone whose origins are rooted in small town America will likely recognize, or be reminded of, characters resembling those written about in this book. My hometown of Carthage, New York, tucked away in the foothills of the Adirondack Mountains, embraces no unique or remarkable attributes that would distinguish it from thousands of such hamlets all across America.

Carthage is a village that reached its maturity in the late nineteenth century. It is a place that was ignored in the post-WWII suburbanization boom, bypassed by superhighways, drained of its young for lack of opportunity, and crippled by the movement of its industry to southern climes. It is precisely because of this history, and the continued migration of its youth, that a cadre of expatriates wistfully remember the quaintness of their hometown and the people among whom they lived.

Former inhabitants of such places—no matter where their migrations take them—carry throughout their lives the memories and traditions that were cultivated and nurtured by their inaugural environments. The alumni of small towns will, as I have often done, affectionately recall, if not dwell on, life as it existed where they grew up.

It would be no exaggeration to say there are billions of untold stories out there that would fill volumes if ever recorded. Each narrative contained herein is inspired by reminiscences that nearly everyone has as they grow older and ponder their past life experiences. The appeal of these pages will surely be found in how and why readers could possibly see themselves and others they know in these particular tales.

Augustinian Academy

1

MY EARLIEST MEMORY AS A CHILD WAS getting my head shaved after returning from a vacation at my Aunt Christine's in Tupper Lake. I was only three but it obviously made a deep impression on me. Vanity, it seems, came early to me. Years later I mentioned this incident to my mother and she remarked that I couldn't possibly have remembered that because I was too young. She became convinced the memory was genuine only when I described where we were living at the time: the end apartment in the Astafan Block on South Mechanic Street.

So why were my brother and I getting our heads shaved? Mother believed that Aunt Christine used too much lard in her cooking and the diet was detrimental to our health, manifesting itself in scalp maladies of one sort or another. This was, no doubt, one of many old wives' tales that passed for home remedies back in the day. In point of fact, I really liked Aunt Christine's cooking. I distinctly remember as a teenager, so voraciously attacking the food she served that she humorously remarked, "Save some for the dog!"

Growing up in Carthage, a small village in Northern

New York, necessarily involved a rather circumscribed focus of activities. It was a time when a relatively small number of families actually owned automobiles and young and old got to wherever they needed the old fashioned way, on foot. Children walked to school, families to church, and housewives to the downtown grocery store to get their weekly supply of vittles. It wasn't uncommon to see young and old on the streets during the daylight and early evening hours, every season of the year. Some who did own cars took them out only for pleasure drives on Sundays. It was a practice that gave rise to the derogatory expression, "He's a Sunday driver," meaning he wasn't very good at it.

Carthage was a one-stoplight, paper mill hamlet with a two-block downtown that housed all the stores and facilities needed to support a population of four thousand people. Among them were a Woolworth's, an A&P grocery, a volunteer fire department, and a police force consisting of a chief and one patrolman. I wouldn't exactly call it a Norman Rockwell setting, but it was virtually indistinguishable from thousands of other small towns scattered across America.

My life revolved around five important venues—home, pop's store, Augustinian Academy, the Boys Club, and St James Church, pretty much in that order. I have fond memories of standing behind the counter of my dad's cigar store when I was only nine, listening intently to my father chat with his customers, competing with my dad to total up the purchases as fast as he did. It was where I got my grounding in arithmetic, the dividends of which would show up early-on in classes at school.

Although I was quite shy by nature, my years behind

the store counter must be credited with the development of my social skills, such as they became. It was a place where I was baptized into the religion of commerce—meeting, greeting, and conversing with people—skills that might have lain dormant otherwise. Pop was a stickler for proper etiquette in dealing with customers—I had to say "good morning" or "good afternoon" to anyone entering the store. I also had to limit discussions to non-controversial subjects such as the weather or who won yesterday's ballgame, and always had to acknowledge receipts of money with a "thank you." I have to confess that I didn't always abide by pop's rules, much to my regret when observed, I might add.

My older sister Theresa and I were pressed into store service at an early age. We often brought pop his lunch or dinner from home, which he would wolf down behind a magazine display rack while monitoring our clerking apprenticeships. He more than once had to lurch out from his impromptu dining room, wiping tahini sauce from his lips, to correct a transaction or answer a question that we didn't understand. But we caught on fast, and later pop was confident enough to begin walking home to get fed, leaving the store completely in one of our capable hands.

It was much later that I began to appreciate the amount of energy and dedication pop expended in providing for his family. Every day of the year he opened his store at 7:00 AM and closed at 11:00 PM He had to be up early to unbundle and display the various morning newspaper bought by customers on their way to work. He would lower the window awning in summer and shovel snow off the sidewalk in winter. It was a relentless schedule

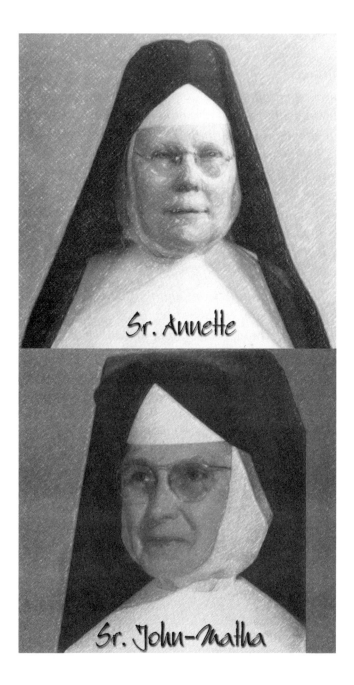

Sr. Annette

Sr. John-Matha

that he pursued diligently, with an indomitable spirit for over fifty years.

The Augustinian Academy became a big part of my life at age four, when I appeared unannounced, trailing after my big brother who was enrolled in the first grade. The first grade teacher was Sister Anette, a kindly woman who showed Job-like patience with me, since I wasn't even supposed to be there. The good sister got tired of sending me home and finally allowed me to audit the class in a back row seat. I think they took pity on my mother who had two more at home younger than I. It would turn out that Sister Anette was the first, and last, teacher to flunk me out. I bawled my eyes out when told that I had to repeat the first grade.

Sister Anita, who inherited the first grade mantle the following year, wasn't as gentle or forgiving, but passed me into the second grade less than two months after my sixth birthday. It was there that I met up with a few of my former classmates who had left me behind the year before. In those days making students repeat grades was not at all frowned upon, and no thought was given to the damage to the self esteem of these students, all of whom would end up dropping out when they reached the minimum age of sixteen.

I really enjoyed my days at Augustinian, although I have to confess that I wasn't much of a student—at least not in the classical sense. My stunted study habits remained underdeveloped throughout my years there, and I generally got by with an innate ability to remember nearly everything that was said in class. Often times I surprised the good Sisters of Saint Joseph with my knack for dumping back on exams the information that I never displayed any knowledge of in class. Sometimes I even surprised myself.

I remember every nun in every grade at Augustinian, some fondly and others not so much, the kind along with the mean, the strict along with the lenient. Sister Siena in the fifth grade sticks out for grabbing me by the hair and rapping my skull against a concrete pillar during recess one day. It still hurts when I think about it, but can't remember what it was that provoked her. As I recall, it didn't take much. Sister St John in the sixth grade is fondly remembered as one of the kindest teachers I ever had. She was a woman who loved both her vocation and children, and it showed. The seventh grade, however, ranks up there as one of the most memorable because that was where I met up with the incomparable Sister John Matha, a woman who, in retrospect, had serious problems—both physical and psychological.

When I began my writing career in earnest, one of the first short stories I wrote was about the seventh grade. It was there for the first time, but alas not the last, that I took to open rebellion against a teacher. Sister Matha believed fervently in the biblical axiom of not sparing the rod, and she administered corporal punishment with unseemly glee. I was often called up to her desk, which sat on an elevated platform, to receive a punishment or two. She would swivel her chair to face me, tell me to hold out my hands and then take a mighty swipe with her rod of choice. Once, as my hands were positioned for punishment, she raised her arm to strike them with her heavy ruler. My athleticism was beginning to bloom, and just as she swung, I adroitly yanked my hands back causing her to strike herself on the knee. That wasn't a clever move because I got hit twice as hard the next time she swung—with her legs prudently tucked under her desk.

One day while walking past my desk, she spontaneously hit me over the head with a geography book. I arose with a start and shouted, "That's it! I'm not taking this anymore!" and thereupon bolted the classroom, running down the stairs two at a time, out the front door, up the alleyway where my bike was parked—still smarting from the blow to the head. I rode around town for awhile, and with no place to go, finally headed towards home, all the while composing a story that would assure my mom that I was the aggrieved party in this latest dispute. On my way home I ran into my classmate Clem who had been dispatched by the startled nun to find and persuade me to come back to school. Clem pleaded with me, "She wants you to come back," he said. I said, "No way! Did you see what she did?" "She wants you to come back," he kept repeating as he stood in front of me with his hands firmly grasping the handlebars of my bike. I finally gave in to Clem's pleadings and returned to school, un-chastened and unrepentant, I might add. Surprisingly Sister Matha, whom I believe realized that she had finally overstepped her bounds, offered no further punishment.

This incident would be the cause of my mother's first appearance at school on my account—and much to my annoyance, actually made me apologize to the nun in front of the class. Talk about blaming the victim. It took several prompts but, I finally gave a begrudging and insincere "Sorry." The good news was that the experience actually had a mitigating effect on the nun's behavior, and she never laid a glove on me for the rest of the year.

This is but one of the memories that inspired me to write the following story about an event that occurred during that school year.

The Seventh Grade

THE FIRST THING THAT STRUCK ME WHEN I went home after being away for a long time was that the old town had shrunk, not only in population but in physical size as well. Everything was smaller, the buildings, sidewalks, and the house where I spent my formative years. While out for a walk one day, I decided to visit the Augustinian Academy to see how it had endured the forty years since I had left.

I walked up the steps of the old three-story brick building, the cornerstone of which said, "Erected in 1885." The old schoolhouse looked every bit its age. It was built the year after a great fire nearly leveled the entire village, save the Catholic Church, which is on a large lot next door to the school. A third story was added in 1906 after another fire partially destroyed the edifice.

In many respects the building resembled a place where one went to for punishment or rehabilitation, lacking only bars on the windows and a guard tower outside. The marble steps leading into the school were worn concave from the hurried footfalls of children dashing in and out over the previous 100 years. I entered the dimly lit hallway to tread upon the not-quite-level maple floors that creaked no matter how lightly kids scampered across them. The place had a faint antiseptic odor, due no doubt to the Sisters of Saint Joseph continually importuning the janitor to mop and clean up. The nuns, who had been charged with the care and intellectual feeding of young Catholic minds of the parish, were neat to a fault and impeccable in their hygienic ablutions.

My memory, it seems, was much larger than the reality that faced me. I had spent twelve years here hustling up and down the stairs, in and out of classrooms, each and every one of which I ambivalently remembered, including the teachers that taught in them. As I crossed the creaky floors, past the third, fourth, and fifth grades, the cubby hole that served as the principal's office came into view at the foot of the stairwell that led to the second floor. While walking up the flight of stairs, my thoughts raced back to the nuns that had instructed me. At the head of the stairs stood the seventh grade. I peered into the small room as a flood of memories engulfed me, memories of a carefree eleven-year-old boy who, until that year, was having the time of his life.

This was the year Peewee McGrath first entered our school. The door opened that fall day, a week after the school term had begun, and there stood a pint-sized, black-haired, long-nosed, skinny kid along with his mother and Sister Camilla, our formidable principal. As his classmates later learned, Peewee had gotten into one scrape too many at the public school, so the Academy became his court of last resort. His mother was at the end of her rope and his father began to believe that a stint in reform school might do the lad some good. In any event, his parents decided to give him one more chance, to see if the nuns at the Academy might be able to do something with him that they couldn't, and the public school teachers wouldn't.

The seventh grade class soon found out what his

frustrated parents knew all too well. Peewee and trouble were constant and willing companions. The boy was the runt of a litter of six children at the McGrath household, and the only male in the brood. His dad was a passive, kindly gent, apparently not the role model Peewee needed amongst all those tall, older, aggressive girls. His home environment seemed to warp his character in ways that caused him to seek attention through reckless daring-do.

Turns out Peewee was actually happy about his transfer to Augustinian because he thought it would provide him with a teacher who wasn't acquainted with his long rap sheet, and he could embark upon a new career of getting away with his brand of mischief. The tall nuns—dressed in long down-to-the-floor black habits, flowing veils, and large circular white guimps that covered any appearance of breasts, leaving only their face and hands showing—scared Peewee not a whit. He could have a lot of fun here he thought, and would have a whole new audience to impress with his wit and trickery. His euphoria, it turned out, was short-lived because his mother personally imparted to the principal a lengthy rundown of the errant student's history.

Peewee was thus enrolled, in what he later called cell block seven, and entered therein to meet his newly appointed jailer, Sister John Matha. Although not eager to have another troublemaker in her charge, the slim, borderline emaciated, hooked on candy, powdery-faced woman in her mid-twenties, felt she was equal to the challenge. A strict proponent of not sparing the rod, she seemed far too delighted when dishing out corporal punishment that, in her mind at least, would eventually tame any miscreant. She was often seen delivering a slap to the side of a boy's head or a crack on his knuckles with a heavy ruler, as I can attest, having been the unlucky recipient on several occasions.

Peewee, however, was one of those boys who was compelled to show everybody that, despite his size, he could do whatever the big boys did. He never backed down from a dare or a fight. One day he took on a kid named Duddy, a bully who was a couple of years older and a head taller than he. Duddy got him down all right, and he wasn't going to get off until Peewee signaled with the accepted "uncle," that he was giving up. Seeing the deck stacked against him, Peewee reluctantly whispered the magic word. He didn't want bystanders to hear him for fear it would brand him a quitter. But it was good enough for Duddy, who had tired of the exercise anyway. However, as soon as he let Peewee up, the little rascal reached up, punched Duddy on the jaw and the fight was on anew. He took a licking, but his pride was still ticking.

It didn't take me long to appreciate Peewee's arrival in the seventh grade, for this had the ancillary effect of giving the good Sister Matha somebody else to hit and holler at besides me. However the boy's reputation for mischievousness was at best understated. He wasn't sassy so much as devious.

For instance, he would turn the wall clock ahead whenever Sister Matha left the room for a candy break, later pointing out that it was time for recess, when it was really fifteen minutes early. This never worked on the beleaguered nun because she kept a tiny pocket-watch pinned to her habit but it gave everyone a muffled laugh. Despite his continued cutting-up, his classmates were not at all prepared for the commotion that Peewee caused a couple of months later.

Fireworks held an especial fascination for Peewee, as they did for most boys that age. It was the time of the big war, and the newsreels were full of bombings and explosions, which were exciting to the patriotic lads who were too young to bear arms. It was also a time of shortages, and amusements of any kind were hard to come by. Truth was, most of us boys, including Peewee, wouldn't have had the money to buy fireworks even if they were available. But the lad was nothing if not resourceful, and was used to making weapons like slingshots from the crotch of a tree branch, or a rubber-band gun out of an old inner tube, a clothespin, with a nail pounded into a piece of wood salvaged from the end of an orange crate.

I never knew if Peewee was the inventor or just an adopter of the ingenious contrivance he told me about in hushed tones one day. "If you cut the tips off kitchen matches," he said as I eagerly listened, "you can use them like gunpowder to make a cherry bomb. I call 'em thunderbolts." We all loved to play with matches, especially those long wooden Lucifers that were hung in containers on the walls of nearly all kitchens of the day. They were mostly used to light kerosene stoves, or to set fire to kindling in cast iron stoves. Many an old man could be seen reaching into his pocket to pull out one, scratch it on the side of his overalls, using it to stoke his pipe. They burned brighter and longer than the cardboard types used for cigarettes and could also be sharpened to be used as toothpicks as well.

"To make one, all you have to do," Peewee continued, "is cut off a few of these match tips and grind them up between two bolts of the same size, screwed together with the right size nut. Throw one of these buggers down on the sidewalk just right, and it'll explode like a firecracker." Peewee, always the zealot when it came to divining pranks, failed to mention that the device could also ricochet up and hit the perpetrator in the eye, which I found out later it sometimes did. Suffice it to say that it was great sport for a seventh grade kid who didn't have access to real fireworks.

It seems there were three major problems with these homemade grenades, and these stumpers continually commanded Peewee's thoughts. The first was the time it took to prepare one. After making a few of these bombs, one got an appreciation of what it must have been like to work a muzzleloader in the French and Indian Wars. And because of misfires and the distinct possibility of premature explosion during manufacture—after all, one had to grind the match heads into powder to make it work—a kid could get tired of this enterprise in a real hurry.

The second problem was the shortage of materials. Peewee was forced to scavenge nuts and bolts from his father's workshop and this proved slim pickings indeed. After all, the war caused so many shortages that the probability of finding matching nuts and bolts in Mr McGrath's tool shed was about the same as finding Sister Matha without a candy stash in her desk.

The third problem was that it didn't take but a few of these nuts and bolts to make a cumbersome load in the bombardier's pockets, which in Peewee's case, in addition to a vial of match heads, were already filled up with important paraphernalia like a jackknife, rabbit's foot, bicycle pants clip, a handful of marbles, and a handkerchief knotted up with a few pennies, just for an emergency.

It plagued Peewee to think that there wasn't a faster way to fabricate these fun makers. After all, a boy with his history had far more candidates to bombard than he could possibly accommodate. For instance, he delighted in sneaking up behind some girl who might have spurned his juvenile advances, and deliver one or two of these missiles at her heels. He hoped to have it ricochet up her dress, thereby extracting a double measure of adolescent revenge—an explosive shock and a spanking, all at the same time.

Since Peewee couldn't carry more than a few of these nuts and bolts at a time, and since he couldn't disassemble and reload them fast enough to satisfy his needs, the bomb-making problem was never far from mind.

One day during religion class, an idea struck him like a bolt of lightning. He suddenly knew how he was going to solve this riddle. Unfortunately the flash occurred when he was supposed to be paying attention to Sister Matha's vivid recitation of the miracle at Lourdes. Maybe there was an inspirational connection, but I could never verify that. Although I had been a collaborator on a few of his capers, I got no advance notice of this brainstorm because the impetuous Peewee decided to try the idea out as soon as it was hatched.

Sister Matha had all her students, except Peewee of course, engrossed in a narration about how the Virgin appeared to Saint Bernadette. Just as Mary made her grand entrance . . . Boom! . . . an explosion rocked the room.

As the momentary screams from the girls and gasps from the boys subsided, all eyes turned toward Peewee and the small mushroom cloud that appeared over his head. Sister Matha, instinctively clutching the crucifix that hung from her neck, lurched from her podium and rushed to the bewildered Peewee's desk, blessing herself three times along the way. Never one who had great presence, especially in times of crisis, the nun grabbed the hapless boy by the ear and stammered "You . . . you . . . get down to the principal's office right now!" To the casual observer, that didn't appear to be the appropriate response for an obviously wounded lad, but it was the best the panicked nun could come up with on short notice.

This of course was not the first time Peewee had been sent to the principal's office. Sister Camilla, the stiff-backed, somewhat haughty woman, who became top nun at Augustinian because of her reputation as a no-nonsense, tough cookie, was never glad to see Peewee, even under the most benign circumstances. And, whenever they met she would assume a stony-faced pose, look down her nose at the hapless miscreant, and threaten to call his parents whose phone number she had unconsciously committed to memory. The ever-present threat of reform school hung heavily in the air whenever Sister Camilla had to discipline the boy. Usually, however, after her invective was spent, she would send him back to his teacher along with a note carrying some prescribed penance.

Unfortunately no matter what contrition was extracted, encounters with Sister Camilla did not to have the desired salutary effect on Peewee. Many times he didn't even go to her office, choosing instead to do time in the lavatory, and after hanging around for an appropriate period, would return to class with the countenance of a choir boy, and a fabricated story about what Sister Camilla recommended. Invariably this included the caveat that he be given another chance. The fact that this over-used act no longer fooled Sister

John Matha never stopped him from trying.

This latest incident however represented a new high in Peewee's misadventures. To say the explosion left the lad in a state of shock is an understatement of significant magnitude. As one who secretly admired the boy's quick wittedness, I had to admit I'd never seen him at such a loss for words. Peewee was dazedly staring at the smoke rising from his left hand. Clem, who sat next to him, claimed that the fireball leapt over his nose while singing his eyebrows and the front part of his hair. A subsequent inspection of the boy's charred features would confirm the power of the blast.

So poor Peewee, clutching his wounded paw like a bear cub with a painful thorn, took leave of the seventh grade. He did not return to class that day and I couldn't stop wondering what happened to him. So after school I went out looking.

When I caught up with him at the Boys Club, his left hand was sporting a bandage the size of a baseball mitt and his face looked and smelled as if it had some kind of salve on it. It turned out that Peewee went neither to the principal's office, nor to the lavatory, but instead to the public health nurse's office. Miss Baldic was a woman with whom Peewee was no stranger, having repaired many of the boy's scrapes from numerous other misadventures. She patched him up and sent him on his way, yet again.

"I had this great idea," he said as he stroked his eyebrows with his good hand, "why not make the chamber loads for the thunderbolts up in advance?" In his musings over the bomb-manufacturing problem, Peewee decided to take the vial of match heads, which was his ordnance inventory so to speak, and literally turn it into a powder horn. He took the cap off the container, and using the eraser end of his pencil, began to mash the match heads into powder. The rest we know. Peewee exploded another, much larger bomb, not up some girl's skirt but in his hapless left hand, which was tightly clutching the miniature fireworks factory. The idea, which came in a flash, left by the same route.

Peewee was neither chastened nor deterred from continuing his schoolboy pranks by this explosive experience. And when his hand healed, he was back at it again. But the predictions of a dire future for the boy, especially by those for whom he had been such a problem, proved to be a bit inaccurate. Several years later, while doing a stint in the Army, Peewee had an epiphany, and after his discharge entered the seminary and became of all things a Catholic priest.

I couldn't help but chuckle as I walked away from the seventh grade.

Sr. Dorothy

2

OBVIOUSLY I WAS HAPPY TO LEAVE THE seventh grade but knew in advance that the eighth would be no picnic. My new teacher, Sister Dorothy, was an elderly nun whose reputation as an exacting educator and disciplinarian was well known and talked about throughout the school. An imposing, if somewhat lean and ghoulish figure, her skin was stretched so taut over her high cheekbones that her face looked like a death mask. She was also one of those nuns who had cultivated a vocal timbre that was calculated to put the fear of God into any student. She also seemed to have eyes in the back of her head and could spot misbehavers with uncanny ability. Unlike her counterpart in the seventh grade, she didn't need, nor was she disposed, to deliver any form of corporal punishment.

On the very first day Sister Dorothy assigned a front row seat to Peewee. She had her ear to the grapevine and knew in advance this student needed closer supervision. The lad took pride in his seat assignment as he interpreted it to be a recognition of his reputation, something of which to be proud.

The eighth grade proved to be full of excitement and

learning, mainly because of Sister Dorothy's love of prose and poetry. She often animatedly recited poems to the class, many lines of which I still remember. One of her favorites was *The Highwayman* by Alfred Noyes. "*Tlot-tlot; tlot-tlot! Had they heard it? The horse-hoofs ringing clear; Tlot-tlot, tlot-tlot, in the distance?*" I believe that onomatopoeic verse was her favorite because she recited it with such gusto.

Sister Dorothy was devoted to her vocation both as a nun and a teacher. Most parochial school students will remember that not only were the rubrics of catechism stressed but so to was spreading the "one true faith." The nun was bent on "saving pagan babies," a cause for which we all were encouraged to raise money. I can still see those little cardboard mite boxes, put out by The Holy Childhood Association, that were used to collect coins for this cause. When the grand sum of $5 was reached, we would "ransom a soul" in darkest Africa, and bestow a given name on him or her. I even had one lucky soul named after me because I raised more money for this cause than the other kids.

One of Sister Dorothy's idiosyncrasies was her hatred for chewing gum. She became quite lathered up when an errant gum-chewer was spotted, and she made the miscreant dispose of it immediately. Alas, you couldn't just take the wad out of your mouth with your fingers. "No, no," she would practically scream, "use a piece of paper!" I don't know why, but touching the gum with your fingers was deemed an unsanitary act, even though it had just been in contact with a more intimate place in your body. Quirks were as prevalent among nuns as they were in the general population.

The eighth grade was where students learned in spite of themselves. Sister Dorothy had lots of spelling bees and made us write many essays. She once chose one of mine, much to my embarrassment, to be read to the class. I thought I was being a wiseacre when I wrote the schmaltzy piece about Jack Frost and his wintry shenanigans. She didn't disclose the author initially and when finished she asked, "Who do you think wrote that?" No one guessed it was me, and when she revealed who it was, as I slouched down in my seat red as a beet, one of boys suggested I had plagiarized it. "Sounds bookish to me," he said. I didn't know if I should have been flattered or insulted.

This was the year that my adventures with Peewee took a more serious turn as he continued to think up newer and more daring pranks. We had to climb all the three-story buildings in downtown, gazing over the edges at all the people passing below. Peewee kept a diary of sorts and vowed to conquer some forty or so structures before he got out of the eighth grade.

There were risks involved in these adventures and they weren't only physical. One time as we were descending from a building that housed an appliance store on the ground floor, a woman darted out of her second story apartment and grabbed me. "What are you doing?" she scolded. "We lost our ball on the roof," I said, "and had to go up to get it." "What's your name?" she demanded. I quickly gave her the name of one of my classmates. "I know your father," she said. "This isn't the last you'll hear of this."

Peewee said, "Boy, that was fast thinking." To me that was high praise from my daredevil pal. I never heard whether the boy I pretended to be ever got reprimanded for my misdeed. Many years later I did tell him about it and he smiled and said, "Yeah, I knew you did that." But he never said he caught hell for it.

One of the problems with Peewee's fertile mind was that each exploit seemed to give birth to continually more daring adventures. Once he saw the view from above, Peewee thought we should take the caper a step further by tossing firecrackers at the hapless strollers below, especially if they were girls we knew. Unfortunately, we didn't have any firecrackers and weren't able to buy any so Peewee's mind raced to find a less costly substitute. The thunderbolts were quickly ruled out because their sheer weight could really cause some damage if they landed on a person's head. "Besides, they probably wouldn't even explode," said Peewee. He then took to rummaging through the garbage cans in the alleys behind the stores and soon found a burnt-out light bulb that one of the stores had discarded. It was of the large, 150 watt, clear-glass variety. "Perfect!" he exclaimed with glee. So up the fire escape we again climbed, crept over to the edge, and awaited our prey. When a couple of girls we knew came by on their way to the malt shop, Peewee dropped the bulb. It made a really large pop, accompanied shortly by the shrieks of the girls. As all eyes from the street turned upward, we beat a retreat to the fire escape.

"Do you think anybody spotted us?" Peewee breathlessly asked. I didn't know because I was in too much of a hurry to leave the scene of the crime to notice. We got away, and even though we were the primary persons of interest in the case, no one actually pinned the deed on us. Sorry to say, it wasn't the last time I participated in that kind of prank as Peewee graduated from light bulbs to eggs and whatever else he thought might be appropriate projectiles. But the next caper is one that reached a new low.

One day, I mentioned to Peewee that I had discovered a practical joke in a comic book involving a paper bag filled with water. What happened next is related in the following story.

The Dirt Bomb

"DON'T READ THE MAGAZINES!" my dad would say. "You'll forget to wait on the customers." He was right of course, but that didn't stop me. For a kid who wasn't terribly interested in school, I read just about anything that was on the racks, except for the comic books, in which I had surprisingly lost interest early on. I didn't think I could learn anything of use in comic books. *Esquire* with those air-brushed Vargas girls was much more to my twelve-year-old liking. They were a lot more attractive than Wonder Woman could ever be. Yet it never ceased to amaze me how interested in comic books many high school boys were. They perused many more than they bought and my dad was always after them to "buy it or beat it."

One day one of my friends was reading a comic that he found highly entertaining and which aroused my curiosity. After he left, I picked up a copy and came across a scene where Jughead filled a paper sack with water and tried to drop it out a window on Archie. According to the comic, when it landed on the sidewalk it exploded with a bang sending water everywhere. I wondered if this was factual or just a fictitious device, like Superman flying, invented to amuse the infantile reader. I had to find out.

The next day, I brought to school a ten pound A&P paper grocery bag from home. I waited until the first recess, took Peewee aside in the boys room, and told him about this marvelous discovery. I proceeded to describe what would happen if we filled this bag with water and dropped it from a reasonable height onto a hard surface.

"I don't believe it," Peewee said. "A bag won't even hold water!" Somehow this prank had escaped his devilish purview and for him, only seeing would be believing. We hung around in the lavatory until alone and then proceeded with the experiment. The room's only window was directly above a basement casement window two stories below, which would give our experiment a good twenty-five foot drop. I carefully filled the sack with water from one of the sink faucets as Peewee's... eyes widened with amazement. The bag held the water without any noticeable leaks. The narrow lavatory window was always open but its sill was five feet from the floor. Only one of us could look out the window at a time so I gave Peewee a boost and he stuck his head out the opening. I gingerly passed the water bomb up to him and while shouting "Geronimo!" he let it fall. A second later a loud bang echoed up from the window well below. "Judas! Water went everywhere!" the excited Peewee exclaimed.

The experiment, now a resounding success, set Peewee's mind spinning with ways to employ this new found technology. "We've got to try this out. We'll drop one of these babies off the top of a downtown building," he said with a mischievous smile. The image of a bag of water exploding atop someone's head played over and over in his brain. Since we had already thrown eggs and light bulbs off these buildings, a bag of water would serve as the *coup de grâce*.

The next day Peewee brought another sack to school for further experimentation. We needed to see how long it would take before the bag started to leak. At the four minute mark, water started to drip out the bottom as the container darkened and absorbed the liquid. Shortly thereafter, it disintegrated as he held it over the sink. "This is going to be a problem, no doubt about it," Peewee muttered.

"Yeah, there's no way we're going to get a bag full of water up a three-story building, is there?" I asked. That was the question, as paper sacks were not equal to the task Peewee had in mind.

"Maybe some old lady in a flat on the top floor will let us fill up on the way to the roof," said he rather facetiously. I suggested we carry a gallon jug of water with us but Peewee rightfully discarded this idea as impractical. Jugs were then made only of glass and would be impossible to take along, given the acrobatics required to mount our objective. No, we'd never make to the top carrying water this way.

Peewee wasn't one to give up easily, and, as was usual with him, thought about it long and hard. A couple of days later when we were in the lavatory, standing in front of the urinals, he announced he had the solution. He then said rather casually, "We're carrying the water with us." It took me a moment to grasp what he was saying. "What we'll do is not pee during the day, and when we get to the top, we'll relieve ourselves in the bag." Sheer genius, I thought, and could hardly hide my admiration for the boy's ingenuity. So the plan was set, the method selected, and the objective identified.

The operation was a go for the next day.

All day long we denied nature's call, crossing our legs to stem the urge. The potential of embarrassing ourselves over this adventure became more and more likely as the day wore on. I didn't go near the lavatory for fear that the sound of a flushing toilet might cause a breach in the dam. Passing the water fountain was equally dangerous as kids slurped and splashed water all over the place. When the final bell signaled that school was over, we virtually flew down the two flights of stairs, out the front door, across the street, and down an alleyway toward our destination.

The building Peewee had selected was a few doors down from the Strand movie theater, directly across the street from the Levis Hotel. This location would surely offer a variety of targets among the many people walking up and down that section of State Street. After arriving at the rear of our target location, I looked up to see a set of porches jutting out that looked like small, rundown tar-paper shacks. A wooden staircase connected each succeeding level, and we quickly scrambled up the steps and made our way to the third floor. At this point we had to mount the railing of the top-most porch and hoist ourselves onto its canopy. Once this maneuver was completed, it was a short step from there to the roof of the building. The effort proved to be more strenuous than usual because we had to crawl over the top of the porch on our bellies. Luckily we managed to make it without spilling any of our bulging cargo.

When we arrived atop the roof, I took out the large sack I'd had brought for the assault, making it ready for arming. Before I could deposit any liquid into the bomb casing, Peewee announced that he had a problem. "I've got to take a crap," he said. "Oh no," I said, "are you going back down?" "Nah, I'll crap in the bag."

I won't go into detail as to what happened next, but the bag was filled with his offal and topped off with our liquid load. With the top duly twisted, it was carried at arm's length to the front of the roof. I was designated bombardier, which entailed my dangling the reeking cocktail over the front of edge of the structure while Peewee scanned the area for potential targets.

"I hope somebody comes along soon," I said. "The sack won't hold this mess very long."

"Don't worry, here he comes now. It's Squirrel Howard. That son of a bitch got me thrown out of the theater one day. Let's get him!" There was no time for discussion as our victim was slowly walking towards the drop zone. Mr Howard, a slight, stooped, shuffling, chain smoking old guy, was the janitor at the Strand Theater. If it could be believed, there was bad blood between Peewee and Squirrel but I wasn't sure if this was really a reason or an excuse. It didn't matter, the bomb was armed and the hapless Mr Howard was in our sights.

Peewee began the countdown. "Five, four, three, two, one," he whispered. "Geronimo!" I let gravity take the bag and then stuck my head over the lip to watch as the projectile headed straight towards the man's head! But just as it passed the second floor, a small current caught it and pulled it in slightly, towards the building. The bag-bomb grazed the left shoulder of the hapless Mr Howard, brushed his side and exploded at his feet, splattering its contents all over his shoes and pants. As soon as it hit, we beat a retreat to the back of the building, over the roof, down the back porches to the first landing, a couple of chortling criminals on the run.

By the time we hit the main drag, we were uncontrollably overcome with laughter. "Boy that was one of the best capers I've been on," said Peewee. "Let's go see the damage."

"We'd better wait a decent interval," said I, not completely sure that someone from across the street, sitting in front of the large plate glass window at the Levis Hotel, hadn't seen us.

"We'll wait fifteen minutes. That ought to be enough," said Peewee. We spent most of our time giggling and when the prescribed interval passed, sauntered down State Street, looking as innocent as a couple of altar boys, which we were by the way. When we arrived at the scene, Jimmy, the proprietor of the grocery store, was busily sweeping the walk. He was laughing as he swept, and his large tummy heaved up and down in rhythm with the broom strokes.

"What's so funny, Jimmy?" I asked.

"You're not going to believe this!" he said. "Osie, you know, the guy who lives up on the third floor? Well, he hates Squirrel Howard with a passion. They're always arguing about something. He just dropped a bag of shit on the old guy!"

We now joined with Jimmy, laughing uproariously, surprised that not only had we been able to pull off a neat prank but had gotten someone else to take the blame. "You're kidding!" we both kept saying.

"No, I'm not," said Jimmy. "Look, here's the spot." At which point he aimed the broom at a dark spot on the sidewalk where he claimed the reeking bomb had landed.

"What did old Squirrel say about that?" Peewee

asked, wanting to savor the whole episode for later retelling.

"Well," said Jimmy, "I heard a loud bang and right afterwards Squirrel came into the store, all the time looking back over his shoulder at a paper bag laying on the sidewalk. He asked for two packs of cigarettes, and all he could say was 'nice day, isn't it?' That's all he said. Had shit and piss all over his pants and shoes. I'm just thankful he didn't get any on the floor."

We all stood there laughing for quite a spell, with Jimmy every so often pausing to look up to make sure that Osie wasn't preparing to launch another shit bomb in our direction. We encouraged Jimmy to retell the story by asking questions such as, "What does Osie have against Squirrel?" And, "Is that all Squirrel said, 'nice day, isn't it'?"

"Osie is a great practical joker," said Jimmy. "Usually his jokes aren't this devious, but he hates old Squirrel. It was him all right. Squirrel used to live below him and they were always fighting about something. I'll never forget the look on old Squirrel's face though. He never knew what hit him (or what just missed him, I thought). I didn't know what happened until I came out to sweep the walk. There it was, shit and piss all over the sidewalk. There's the spot and that's the bag over in the gutter!" Jimmy so delighted in retelling the story that we could see he had been provided with several days' amusement with which he could regale his friends and customers.

Four years passed before I got up the nerve to tell Jimmy the true story. "Sure, sure," he said. "You and Peewee. Right, right. Next you'll be telling me Osie loved Squirrel, right?" He had told the story so many times to so many people that the tale was indelibly etched in his mind.

Who said truth is stranger than fiction, or that you can't learn anything from comic books?

The Island Paper Mill

3

WHEN I LOOK BACK AT THAT ADVENTURE, I have
to admit I'm embarrassed to even tell the tale.
Although this is not offered as an excuse, I'm describing
the antics of a couple of twelve-year-old boys, given
to extremely adolescent behavior, in a town that was
starved for entertainment venues for kids that age. Our
surroundings also gave rise to quite foolish behavior,
behavior that would go so far as to endanger our lives.

Working at my father's store gave me a chance to
observe and converse with his many customers, which I
truly enjoyed. Harry Walts, a teller at Carthage National
Bank, was one of those whom I found quite interesting.
He drove in from Watertown for his job every business
day and usually arrived well before the bank opened.
Harry would wait for the appointed hour at pop's store,
usually just staring out the front window at the bank
across the street. He was the most impeccably dressed
teller you'd ever want to meet. He even wore spats over
his shoes and always had a handkerchief in his breast
pocket. Harry prided himself on his penmanship and
would show me how to make various letters with bold
flourishes. I practiced my signature with the ornate
hieroglyphs Harry made, and still use it today.

One time, when the bank was closed for business, he took me with him to see what the teller cages were like on the inside. Behind every teller's cage, dusty revolvers were nestled in compartments underneath. They obviously hadn't been used in a long time, so I asked Harry if they were loaded. "Oh, yes," he said. I can't imagine that the bank paid their tellers enough to put up a fight if ever a robbery was in progress. Soon I had a vision of old Harry staggering out of the bank with blood spattered across one of his fancy suits.

I wasn't the only one who wondered how Harry could afford his late model Chrysler and his fancy clothes on a teller's salary. That, however, would always remain a mystery.

Beanie Baker was another of the characters who was a regular at pop's store. He enjoyed telling stories that could embellish his reputation as the town's philosopher. Ever trying to sound profoundly intellectual, Beanie would spin his yarns with an all-knowing voice. Whenever two or three were gathered, he would reach into his repertoire and fish out a canard or two.

One day Beanie tried to impress us with a tale about a man he knew who had successfully invented a perpetual motion machine. During the late nineteenth century heyday of American mechanical inventiveness, a great many tinkerers were enamored with the notion of creating a machine that could produce work without inputting any additional energy. Of course such a contraption would violate the first and second laws of thermodynamics, but that didn't deter them—and probably wouldn't have even if they were aware of those laws of physics.

"Got it working okay," Beanie said, "and all he had to do was make it run faster. So he took it apart and tinkered with some of its parts and then put it back together. Couldn't ever make it run again."

I remember, many years later, when I was managing an engineering group and the designers were faced with the retooling of a computer part, I said rather spontaneously, "Yep, all we have to do is make it run faster." I chuckled, because the engineers didn't have a clue as to what I was talking about. I was simply trying to make the point that after they got it back together, it might not work at all.

Beanie also delighted in telling me how he happened to be present on the day that my dad got into an altercation about the pinball machines that graced the rear of the store. Leo, the man who serviced those machines, was a former noted athlete and police chief at one time in our town. His fortunes had declined, largely because he had gotten involved in some shady dealings, the exact details of which I never knew. The way the pinball deal worked was that the store got half the money that the machines took in, which came mostly from high school kids.

Leo was charged with counting and sorting the nickels that the machines yielded. For some reason my dad became suspicious that he was being short-changed. One day, after Leo turned over the store's share, pop brushed up against Leo and tapped his coat pocket with the back of his hand. Not surprisingly, at least to him, he felt a pocket bulging with coins. An altercation ensued, and according to Beanie, he had to intervene before any serious harm was done.

My dad reported this incident to the pinball company that provided the machines, and we never saw Leo again.

But, my adventures with Peewee were destined to continue, and before we got out of eighth grade, he would persuade me to continue pushing the envelope of foolhardiness. One of my most memorable escapades is recounted in the following story.

Dam Foolishness

GOD MADE THE COUNTRY, MAN MADE the city, but the Devil made the small town," was Beanie Baker's pronouncement one day in my dad's store. I don't know if it was a consequence of the Devil's architecture, but small towns seem to have an abundance of odd characters. Carthage, New York, certainly was no exception. There were, of course, the usual set of panhandlers and drunks, I would guess in the same numerical proportion as in other towns and cities. I remember one such besotted beggar in particular who did not take kindly to rejection of his entreaties. If refused a handout, he would shout for all to hear, "I can buy and sell you with the loose change in my pocket!" Another eccentric walked around with a parrot perched on his shoulder, mumbling incoherently to the squawking bird while completely indifferent to the trail of white droppings that streaked down the back of his coat. I always assumed, because of the parrot and the faded tattoo on his arm, he was a crazy, bird-loving, old salt, but I never knew for sure.

Beanie Baker was the town philosopher—a title neither earned nor complimentarily bestowed. Not observably gainfully employed, he had lots of leisure time to wax eloquently about life, and he had an opinion on just about everything. Although his given name was DeWitt, everybody called him Beanie, a tart tribute to his pseudo-intellectual stream of gratuitous pronouncements that came from his bean. The man spent his days standing on a corner of State Street, puffing on a large cigar, while casting a wary eye on all the comings and goings of the town. Always dressed in a checkered wool shirt, jodhpurs and high-top boots, summer and winter, he rarely smiled. But when he did, a prominent gold tooth punctuated his parted lips.

The most famous of the village's characters, however, was Waldo Pratt; at least I thought his name was Waldo because that's what Beanie always called him. Mr Walter Pratt was an honest to goodness gentleman millionaire, famous or infamous depending on your point of view, as the owner the now defunct Island Paper Mill. Back in 1932, Pratt had threatened he'd close his mill if the Democrats got in and right after Franklin Roosevelt was elected, he did just that. The Island Mill had lain fallow ever since, and only Pratt's watchman could be seen there, making his monotonous rounds of the ghostly mill.

Virtually all the town's characters frequented my dad's cigar store, a place where I spent many hours tending trade. Mr Pratt visited only during the summer months and stayed at the Grand Union Hotel. While in residence he would come into the store every morning to buy *The New York Times*. This was right after he'd had breakfast up the street at Fuhrken's Diner. Mr Pratt was a man of few words, and he grunted a lot. Economy of words, it seems, only accentuated his famed frugality, which slightly exceeded his obvious eccentricity. Many people, including Beanie, claimed to know stories about Mr Pratt. Beanie often liked to repeat a story about old "Waldo" making his watchman pay for repairs to the time-clock he used on his rounds. "Wasn't even his fault it broke!" he added with disgust.

Eddie, the proprietor of the diner where Pratt had breakfast every morning, also attested to Pratt's parsimony whenever he came in to buy his usual nickel bag of Bull Durham. He'd tell how Mr Pratt would get the breakfast special, two donuts and coffee, eat one and wrap the other up in a napkin to take with him. "Imagine that!" Eddie said indignantly. "The old tightwad wouldn't want anybody else to get that donut!" We, of course, had to ignore the fact that Eddie was spending only five cents on a sack of Bull Durham to roll his own, rather than fifteen cents on ready-made cigarettes.

Mr Pratt was the best-dressed old geezer in town. In sharp contrast to Beanie's lumberjack look, he wore impeccably tailored, worsted wool suits with silk ties knotted under a stiff celluloid collar. In his breast pocket was a pair of pince-nez reading glasses that were attached to a black ribbon, pinned to his lapel. The tall, lean gentleman cut quite a figure for someone I guessed to be approaching sixty.

Whenever Beanie encountered Pratt in my dad's store he would always address him deferentially as "Mr Pratt," but all I ever heard was a grunt for a reply. I got the impression that old man Pratt wasn't comfortable speaking to someone as far down the social ladder as Beanie Baker, philosopher or not.

Most people offered old man Pratt a deferential nod and gave way when passing him on the street. Other than a cursory "Hello" there wasn't much exchanged in the way of conversation.

My friend Peewee, however, was never in awe of money or authority. Whenever he saw Mr Pratt in the store, he would go right up to the old gent and start quizzing him. "Are you really a millionaire?" Pratt, whose attention to *The New York Times* financial page was painfully interrupted, would peer down over his pince-nez glasses and grunt, regarding Peewee as an unpleasant insect or a noxious odor that had invaded his personal space. "Are you ever going to reopen the mill?" Peewee would continue. To which Pratt would mutter, "These ruffians have no respect for their elders these days," or some such rejoinder that old folks use when talking about the younger generation.

After Pratt took his leave, Beanie Baker would gain his voice and launch into a denigration of the man. "What a cheapskate Waldo is," he would say. "He squeezes a nickel so tight that the Indian is riding the buffalo." He would then give out a snicker at his homespun humor and repeat to anyone within earshot the story of Pratt's watchman. "Wasn't even his fault it broke!" he'd say again.

One day after Mr Pratt had left the store, Peewee suggested that the defunct Island Mill would be a good place to go exploring. "We can have a lot of fun there," he said, "but we'll have to be on the lookout for the watchman." It seems Peewee had been caught at the mill before and since the watchman knew who he was, didn't want to be seen, much less get caught again.

I was more than a little skeptical about Peewee's proposed adventure. It wouldn't be good for me to get on Pratt's bad side because he'd be sure to tell my dad, and then I'd catch it but good. Like the time pop caught me ice skating in my overshoes on the frozen Black River down by Pratt's mill. It wasn't just that I couldn't swim, as if that would have mattered in the dead of winter, it was that everyone knew that the river had laid claim to many a foolhardy kid, year in and year out. I didn't look forward to another bout with dear old dad about playing down by that treacherous stream.

From time to time nearly all the boys of the village frolicked on the shores of the Black River. They waded in it, skipped stones over its surface, or even tried to catch its fish. Being a non-swimmer didn't stop me either because the river drew kids to its bosom like a crying baby to its mother. So as usual, I consented to explore the Island Paper Mill with Peewee that day.

We walked down Mechanic Street to the railroad station, crossed the tracks and sauntered over to a siding that would lead us to the mill. The old factory, true to its name, was on an island that was reached by crossing a short bridge near the railroad track. The span itself, in surprisingly good shape for its lack of maintenance, was a single steel arch with a wooden plank deck about fifty feet long.

Now full of anticipation at our adventure, we scampered across the bridge, and before anyone could see us, made our way around to the back of the property, carefully avoiding the sightline of the watchman's shack. The island was quite large and had a fair sized Victorian mansion on it, as well as the large paper making facility. The house, originally occupied by the mill owner, had long ago been converted to an administrative building. There was also a huge garage where a half-dozen old automobiles were stored. It seems Mr Pratt never sold or traded-in his cars, preferring to hang on to them, thereby enhancing his reputation for eccentricity.

Fancying ourselves as modern-day versions of Lewis and Clark, we surveyed our way over the site to the south side of the island, and circled round a big brick structure that contained the main paper processing equipment. The plant hugged the shoreline and immediately behind it lay a narrow channel of the river and another island, a tiny spit of land whose dense foliage obscured the main body of the river. A small dam, about 20 feet long, connected the larger island to the smaller one. The water gently flowing over it was shallow, and in combination with sunny skies, provided a tranquil scene for the day's adventure.

Peewee, buoyed by the balmy weather and his natural reckless spirit, decided that it would be great fun to wade across the weir, to cool our tootsies as it were. So we took off our shoes and socks, tied the shoelaces together, slung them around our necks, and like a pair of yoked oxen began sloshing around on the little dam. The cool water, gently flowing over the barrier, barely reached our ankles and the moss covering was smooth and refreshing to the soles of our feet. The water on either side of the little dam wasn't very deep either— three feet at most.

"This is a lot of fun," I exclaimed. But no sooner had I gotten the words out of my mouth than a loud shout echoed in the distance behind us. We looked to see Mr Pratt's watchman coming towards us on the run. "What are you boys doing there?" he barked. "Come back here before I call the police!"

Peewee, ever prepared for a quick retreat, darted over to the companion island to escape the onrushing watchman. Without hesitation, I found myself close behind. The journey to the smaller land mass was accomplished in record time and when it was reached, we continued running through the brush around small trees to its western boundary. Now, at least, we weren't visible to our pursuer even though he was only a short distance away.

The man continued shouting at us from across the water. "Come back here," he called. "I'll be waiting for you!" Luckily, he'd decided to halt his pursuit at the small dam.

I turned to see where we were and the sight literally took my breath away. The main dam, which looked to be at least a thousand feet long was spilling water over its edge at a pretty good clip, unlike its sister barrier upriver that I also knew. It was in the waning days of spring, and the river had not yet completed its normal summer recession. The dam was about eight feet high and the mist caused by the falling water mostly obscured the view to the other side of the river.

"What are we going to do now?" I shouted over the roar of the waterfall. Peewee, a veteran of many scrapes said, "Hey, we'll go across to the other side. He can wait for us till hell freezes over. We're not going back that way."

I was now on the horns of a dilemma, afraid to go back and afraid to go forward. "Old man Pratt's going to tell my dad," I yelled.

"Nah," Peewee said. "The watchman didn't get close enough to recognize us. Besides, what choice do we have?" The logic wasn't lost on me so I gritted my teeth and prepared to follow Peewee across the great divide.

In the lead and now impatient for action, Peewee quickly darted on to the precipice. Hesitantly I hollered, "Are you sure we can make it?"

"Yeah, it's easy," he answered. "I've done it many times."

Mindful of Peewee's reputation as a daredevil and also as one given to an occasional boast or two, I was not assured that the intrepid explorer had indeed negotiated this particular obstacle before. Nonetheless, and with no little apprehension, I followed. At first, as with most misadventures that are later regretted, it didn't appear all that difficult. Near the shore the water seemed neither swift nor deep, and the ledge upon which I began the journey, although a little slick, was about two feet wide. The water however, was a lot higher than on the smaller dam we had just crossed, as it was well over my ankles at the beginning.

Peewee was having a ball, and quickly drawing away from me towards the opposite end of the dam. I tried as best I could to keep up but the creeping apprehension I felt was rapidly turning to outright fear. The boiling mass below to my right didn't look any too hospitable even if I could swim. To make matters worse, the misting spray was beating a path up my nostrils as the water edged its way up my shins to my knees! I tried not to look down because the swirling water made me dizzy. Yet I was afraid not to look down for fear of losing my footing, so I compromised by guiding on Peewee who was now about ten feet ahead of me. My companion was oblivious to my plight as he sashayed over the slippery concrete precipice while whistling as loudly as he could.

I began to consider, as the good nuns at Augustinian had taught me to do in times of peril, asking for divine intervention. Remorseful thoughts began coursing through my brain, like how stupid I was; how I wished I had led a more exemplary life; how I should've listened to my dad about playing by the river; how no kind of punishment was worth avoiding for this stupid escape plan. And, how I would like to kill Peewee if I lived through this ordeal.

Doomed to completion of the task because I was too afraid to turn back, I kept edging my way across the dam. The roar of the water drowned out Peewee's whistling along with any reproach I could have delivered. So now, thoroughly frightened, I continued sliding and praying my way across the fool dam, wondering if Peewee would jump in to save me if I fell, and if it would do any good if he did.

Finally, in what seemed an eternity, we reached the other side. I was torn between cussing out Peewee and thereby letting him know how terrified I was, or acting blasé in the rush of relief that inevitably follows a narrow escape. I decided on the latter course while reflexively breathing a tremendous sigh. My joy proved to be premature and short lived. Much to my dismay, at the western terminus of the dam was an outcropping of rock that anchored it to a narrow channel of deep, rapidly rushing water, over which there was no way to shore.

"How are going to get back now?" I fairly pleaded. "Simple," said Peewee, who seized the opportunity to play on my obvious fear. "We'll walk back across the dam after the watchman is gone."

"Like hell!" said I, no longer worried about Mr Pratt or his watchman but instead feeling a much more acute concern for my personal safety. "I'll starve out here on these rocks first," I said.

"All right," Peewee said. "Then we'll just go upriver." As luck would have it, the rock that I was ready to call home opened up to a wide expanse of exposed limestone that formed a large island in the river. This rock bed reached all the way upstream to the dam below the bridge that connected Carthage to its western sister. I decided, given the circumstances, to follow my latter day Moses once more, hoping to finally be led to the Promised Land.

We made our way up to the mentioned dam, which had no water cascading over its rim. To my undying relief, Terry, a river rat I knew was fishing nearby, and had beached his father's boat on the lip of the dam. "How the heck did you get here?" he asked.

"We're, ah . . . we've been, ah . . . exploring," I stammered. "Could I catch a ride back with you?"

"Sure," Terry said, and I breathed a second and final sigh of relief. My prayers had been answered!

Peewee, whose appetite for adventure was as yet unsatiated, decided he would explore some more by himself. Meanwhile, my savior and I began paddling back upstream from the dam. Which route Peewee took back home I never knew nor asked, because I was not at all certain I would get the truth anyway. And, Mr Pratt never said anything to my dad.

But this was a harrowing experience that I will remember to my dying day. I dream of it often.

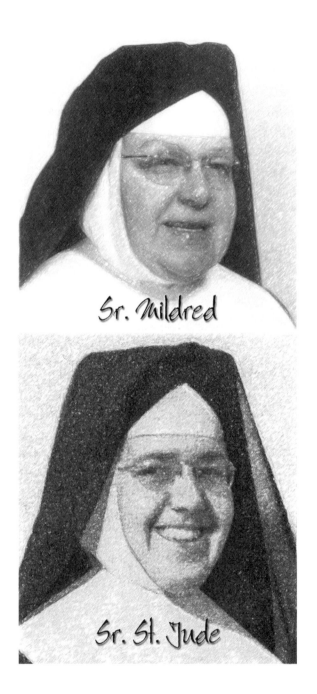

Sr. Mildred

Sr. St. Jude

4

HIGH SCHOOL AT AUGUSTINIAN ACADEMY was in the same building and only a few steps away from grade school. Unlike the campus schools of today, all twelve grades were contained in one large building, housing three hundred students on three floors. There were no separate buildings for elementary, junior or senior high. Yet students embraced a feeling of having made it when they passed through that imaginary portal from eighth grade to first year of high school. This was where we would get our first exposure to different teachers for different subjects. We were also now joined by several new kids who rode the bus from surrounding villages that were too small to have high schools of their own. The newbies came from Natural Bridge, Herrings, Deferiet, and a few one-room schoolhouses out in the country. Thus, we soon became acquainted with several kids we had never known before.

One of the new guys, a kid named Jack from Herrings, always had a smart-aleck answer for everything, much to the teachers' dismay and my delight. In algebra class one day, when Sister St Jude asked him where his book was, he replied, "Why between its covers, I suppose." Needless to say, Jack became unpopular with the teachers but quite a hit with guys like Peewee and me.

Sister St Jude was not a well-liked nun. She was a tense woman who wasn't really cut out for teaching, especially in high school. She wore thick glasses on a rosy round face that turned deep red at the smallest provocation, and her mouth always had a bubble of spittle gracing its right corner. Sister St Jude's goat was on a very short leash and could be summoned almost on command by any errant student. If ever there was a candidate for apoplexy, she would have been elected by a landslide.

My favorite teacher in high school was my math instructor Sister Mildred, whom I thankfully inherited after barely passing Sister St Jude's algebra. Sister Mildred was probably the main reason I graduated high school because she greatly motivated me, even though for the life of me I can't remember why or how. I just loved the way she taught mathematics, which ended up becoming my major in college. Sister Mildred was a large woman of German stock from an old Pittsburgh family by the name of Coon. The diabetic nun exhibited all the signs of high blood pressure on her pinkish countenance and was usually short of breath after climbing the stairs to class. Nonetheless, she was a woman who exhibited wisdom far greater than that of the principal, Sister Camilla, who also was from Pennsylvania.

One time, when Sister Camilla suspended me from classes, Sister Mildred was obviously displeased. "I don't see what good that's going to do," she muttered when I gave her the news as to why I'd be missing her class. She didn't say anything directly against Sister Camilla, but she didn't have to. The reason I got suspended, by the way, was because of an altercation I had with the principal that began innocently enough as I was sitting in study hall, reading a book. Sister Camilla was pulling double duty teaching her social studies class on one side of the room, and acting as study hall monitor on the other. It was in the latter duty that she decided to look at the calendar on her desk and noticed a notation that I had been late for school again that morning. Even though we lived only a block away, I seemed always to find a way to be a few minutes late.

"Mr Ellis," she barked, interrupting her class, "I see you were late again this morning. Can you explain why?" Frankly, I was not only taken by surprise, but also exceedingly annoyed for being singled out for attention, especially since I was actually doing school work for a change. After regaining my composure, I instinctively took a page out of Jack's book and said, "I suppose because I didn't get here on time." I think I may even have added a tinge of sarcasm to my response, but at this juncture I'm not sure.

Sister Camilla promptly blew a fuse, which in retrospect she might have been allowed to do, given my response. "You get your cap and coat and come up here mister," she barked. She then took out a card from the desk drawer and began to furiously write upon it. Feeling equally put out, I rose with such abruptness from my stand-alone desk that it toppled over with a loud bang. I left the desk in its new state of repose as I slowly retreated to the cloak room to retrieve my coat. There was no cap because my jackets always had hoods to shield me from winter weather. When I came back by my desk, I paused, stared down at it for a few seconds, and then decided to right it rather than press the issue any further.

Sr. Camilla

Sr. Bernadette

When I reached the principal's desk she growled, "You take this note to the pastor immediately!" Her words marched out in a quite unfriendly cadence, fairly dripping with authority.

The church and its rectory are next door to the school, as mentioned before, so it's but a short walk to get over there. I admit I was fuming as I walked out of school and sauntered up the sidewalk leading to the rectory. I noticed that Sister Camilla in her haste and anger had forgotten to seal the envelope, so I took the liberty of reading the charges against me.

"This boy has been consistently impertinent, and I recommend that he be expelled from school and kicked off the basketball team." I couldn't help but notice the anger in her pen strokes as I returned the card to its proper place while wondering if the old gal hadn't got things in the wrong order. Once I got kicked out of school, I wouldn't have been eligible to play basketball anyway.

I apprehensively rang the doorbell to the rectory. "Yes," the housekeeper answered. "I'm here to see Father Egan," said I. "Sister Camilla wants me to deliver this note to him." She bade me come in, went over to the staircase and pressed a bell-button on the wall. I could hear a buzzer signal for the priest's attention and shortly a loud, "Yes," came tumbling down from above. "The Ellis boy is here with a note from school," she said. There was a pause, then the gruff and obviously annoyed voice spoke again, "I'll be down shortly." I got the feeling I had caught the old priest at a bad time, perhaps performing his morning constitutional, and this wouldn't be a good time for me to be bearing bad news.

After a few minutes, Father Egan, a heavy-set man of about sixty, lumbered down the steps and motioned with a grunt for me to follow him into his office. I handed him the note as he took his seat behind his large desk. I knew Father Egan liked me because I often served him as his altar boy and he was always kind to me. He also came into the store occasionally and was friendly with pop. Now, however, his expression betrayed some annoyance as he read the note's contents, and then let out a sigh. "Well young man," he said, "you've done it this time. I guess I'm going to have to send you home."

My brain was racing to supply a plausible defense and quickly came up with the following line of attack. "Well Father," I said drawing my words out slowly, "I don't think my mother is going to like that. Remember the last time?" A pained expression raced across Father Egan's furrowed brow, stopping dead center to fester there. "Hmm," he said as he slowly replayed in his mind previous encounters with my mother. "Perhaps, on second thought, we better not do that." Mom had a reputation for speaking up, priest or not, and although she permitted the school to discipline me in any way they saw fit, she had but one condition—"Just don't send him home," she said.

Finally, the priest began scribbling a note on the back of the offending card, which he then replaced in the envelope, licked and sealed the flap. "Give this back to the principal," he said with a frown, "and you'd better bring me your basketball jacket." "Rats," I thought, " I'm off the team." And I wouldn't even be able to read what he'd written.

When I returned the note to Sister Camilla, she

quickly ripped it open, scanned the contents, and began to seethe. I actually thought I saw steam escaping from under her wimple—that stiff white cowl that framed her face, covered her ears, and circled under her chin. "Well," she fumed, "you are suspended from classes until further notice!" And, that's how I got put into Camilla's purgatory, and Sister Mildred didn't like it. The banishment lasted three days before the principal saw the futility of her pique.

On the following Friday, before our weekly basketball game, I went over to the rectory to plead my case for reinstatement. "It's the Ellis boy again," shouted the housekeeper up the stairwell. "The jacket's in the hall closet," boomed the voice from above. Father Egan liked basketball and I couldn't help but think that he thought our chances of winning would be better if I was playing. I breathed a sigh of relief—I was back on the team.

My writing career actually began in my senior year when I was named sports editor of our class yearbook. I really enjoyed sports reporting and actually began to think of this as a career option. However my academic record, other than for mathematics, wasn't exactly stellar and wouldn't have recommended me for many intellectual careers. In fact, after I began counting up my credits for graduation, I found that I'd be a half credit short of the required sixteen. In a bit of a panic, I stopped in to see the diminutive and amiable Sister Bernadette, the business subjects teacher. If there had been a popularity contest for the nuns, I think Sister Bernadette would have won hands down. "How about I take typing?" I asked. "It's already February and this is a one year course," she replied. I took her through the

"The Pest Guest" – Senior Play

arithmetic of my needing another half credit so she reluctantly allowed me to join her class. I was put off in a corner in front of a typewriter and valiantly tried to follow along and catch up. I distinctly remember the first speed test a couple of weeks later, and after totaling up my score, I asked Sister Bernadette if nineteen words per minute was good. She tried to hide her anguish and said that it was "alright." When I took the Regents exam in June, I finished with an eighty-eight and had enough credits to graduate.

Ever the wiseacre, I wrote an article for the yearbook about my pal Peewee McGrath. It was titled *My Favorite Senior.*

> My ideal senior is Peewee McGrath. He is a stellar example of honest study and fortitude. He is loved by nuns and students alike for his charming personality and suave manner. Hour after hour he labors through the day at his lessons never complaining never flinching. His stay at the Academy has been enriched by intense study and his admirable love for learning. With the faculty he has attained dear friends who will remember him throughout life for the kindness he has shown them. He has gained an especially dear friend in our principal who is at all times ready to defend him against all who would besmirch his good name. So, we say to you Peewee, farewell and good luck.

I was actually surprised that the nuns accepted the piece for publication, although they edited it a bit. I had a line in it that claimed that Peewee was "endowed with a cephalic ganglion the like of which no man hath." I think that sounded off-color even though it was just a fancy way of saying he had a unique brain.

The good sisters were always putting on plays and pageants, and a somewhat prophetic happenstance occurred when Sister Mildred cast me in the lead in the senior play, The *Pest Guest*. The story was about a novelist, the bearded Randolph Stottard, alias Jack Carlton, who made a real nuisance of himself while visiting at the celebrity conscious Bradford family home. It was quite similar to the movie that starred Monty Woolley as *The Man Who Came to Dinner,* which was based on the Kaufman-Hart play by the same name. I don't know why, but Sister Mildred was always pushing me into activities like plays and the choir.

In the years after high school, I had many occasions to visit the Sisters of Saint Joseph's motherhouse to call on my sister Theresa, who had joined the order. The last time I saw my favorite nun, Sister Mildred, she couldn't even recognize me. What a shame, I thought, such a brilliant mind locked up in her own private prison. My old nemesis, Sister Camilla, had become wheelchair bound and she had also developed severe dementia. On a bright sunny day, not too long after my last visit, one of the nuns was looking out the window and saw Sister Mildred pushing Sister Camilla's wheelchair down the long expanse of driveway leading from the motherhouse to the very busy highway. In a panic, she ran down the driveway, and when she caught up to them she asked, "Sisters, where are you going?" "To Pittsburgh," they both announced. How sad.

I've reflected on those years often and when I began writing, the following true experience quickly came to mind.

The Game of Life

NOT ALL THE KIDS KNEW THAT VINNIE's given name was actually Vincenzo. The curly haired, seventeen-year-old with sharp features accentuated by high cheekbones was the unquestioned star of Augustinian Academy's basketball team, and its senior class president. To me, a thirteen-year-old aspiring ballplayer, Vinnie was the one I would most like to emulate. I even coveted the jobs Vinnie had—working at the Boys Club and ushering at the Strand Theater. I dreamed of having those jobs one day—playing basketball and seeing movies for free—and getting paid for it too. It just didn't get much better than that.

Whenever I could get away from working at my father's store, I literally haunted the Boys Club—especially the gymnasium. The Club was a godsend for kids like me. It was on the second and third floors of an old downtown business building, and had game rooms, a poolroom for boys sixteen and older, a woodworking shop, and even a small print shop that produced periodic bulletins about Club activities. I signed up for the print shop and learned how to set type and run the small printing press, which was great fun.

The gym was located on the third floor and was where I got my first taste of the game of basketball. Augustinian had no gymnasium so the Boys Club let us use their gym for practice. I was a freshman in high school and been playing basketball at the Club since seventh grade.

The Academy's varsity players were regulars at my dad's store, and I enjoyed chatting with them, even though I was as much as five years younger than they were. I had become quite at ease conversing with older boys. I read the newspapers regularly and could talk about things my elders were interested in, such as the war and professional sports. pop's store, which was across the street from the school, had become a high school hangout and Academy kids regularly came in to buy candy, soda pop, comic books, and to play the pinball machines.

Whenever I got a chance, I'd sidle up to Vinnie at the Boys Club and ask him to show me some of his basketball dribbling tricks. He was an extremely good ball handler. "C'mon kiddo," he would say. "Not like that, like this!" as he bounced circles around me.

Another guy I got to know well was Vinnie's classmate and best friend, Jimmy. They hung around together a lot, which seemed strange because they were poles apart in appearance and athletic ability. Vinnie was tall and slender, and had an alertness about him that bespoke intelligence. Jimmy was no athlete and was affectionately called "Skinny" by just about everyone, including his friend Vinnie. He had a head shaped like a pumpkin that sat atop his two hundred plus pound body, one that was totally unsuited for sports. Perhaps if our school had a football team, which it didn't, Jimmy might have made a good lineman. However, the closest he got to athletics was as basketball team manager and scorekeeper. Perhaps it was Jimmy's way of supporting his friend Vinnie. The differences in looks and athleticism didn't seem to affect their friendship at all.

I liked Jimmy because he could converse about many different things. He was seriously interested in photography, which also intrigued me. Occasionally, he'd let me observe as he developed pictures in the small basement darkroom under his father's Italian grocery store. Jimmy took pictures of Vinnie playing basketball, which he developed, enlarged and pasted up on his darkroom wall, alongside a girl he was smitten with, but who never gave him the time of day.

My love of basketball continued despite not making the junior varsity traveling team, and I eagerly looked forward to going to our school's basketball games. Whenever the team traveled to places such as Tupper Lake, Ogdensburg, Watertown, or Antwerp, I was sure to be on the bus. The trips were long, and we got home late, but that only added to the pleasure of it all.

The school hired buses for our away games, and for fifty cents students could ride along with the players, cheerleaders, and chaperones. The buses were always crowded but I never minded, apart from the price, because being part of a festive group, out from under the watchful eyes of the Sisters of Saint Joseph, was a lot of fun.

When outward bound, the boys sat in the back of the bus and the girls in front. The return trip was a different matter however, as the chaperones were either too tired to notice or didn't care that boys and girls had paired up in the darkness. High school romances were in full bloom on bus trips heading home. Although I loved the trips, I had no desire to pair up with a girl, or a girl to pair up with if I did. I always watched to see who Vinnie might sit with but, even though the cheerleaders flirted openly with him, he always ended up with his friend Jimmy as his seatmate.

One problem that nagged me was the fifty-cent tab for the trips. I have to admit that I somewhat begrudgingly coughed up the fare because I not only loved basketball, but wouldn't want to miss seeing Vinnie play. I earned my bus fare by peddling newspapers or, when desperate, begged from my dad. That was why, on the day before the Antwerp game, I listened intently when Peewee suggested a way to make the trip without paying.

Now Peewee was nothing if not observant—and conniving. "You know," he said, "they always count the kids going out but never on the way back. If we could get to the game somehow, we could sneak on to the bus for the trip home." This bit of chicanery would never have occurred to me, and I had to concede that Pewee had a good point—if we could get to the game, that is.

"We'll hitchhike!" Peewee announced with his usually omnipresent ring of authority. Normally we wouldn't have considered this a prohibitive distance for thumbing a ride but on that winding highway during the dead of winter, it would present a fairly significant challenge. We frequently hitched rides during the summer months, and we knew the roads around the village pretty well. But, it was February and plenty cold out, with temperatures often dipping to twenty below zero after the sun went down.

As with most of Peewee's schemes, I was more than a tad skeptical, and justifiably so, considering the scrapes we'd gotten into in the past. With this daredevil, it was always hard to tell where bravery ended and foolhardiness began—where cunning and intelligence gave way to excess and folly. But as usual I would go along with his daring scheme. After all, fifty cents was a great deal of money, and I wouldn't want to miss seeing

Vinnie play.

On the afternoon of the game, I rushed out of the house having fibbed to my mom that I was taking the school bus to the basketball game. I met up with Peewee and we quickly headed out to the village limits. After sticking our thumbs out, we soon got a three-mile ride to Fargo's Corners, a place where the road forked, forcing travelers to choose between the more heavily used Route 3 and the less traveled road that would take us to Antwerp. A farmer driving a flatbed truck stopped and motioned for us to hop on the back. A few hundred feet later we were sorry for accepting this Samaritan's gift because as the arctic air washed over the cab at fifty miles an hour, we shivered and froze in the open air. It took two more rides, spaced between barely bearable frigid interludes, to put us in front of the Antwerp high school—just before our school bus was scheduled to arrive.

Desperate to warm up, we eagerly went inside—to the accompaniment of strange looks from the locals who were expecting a much larger contingent of visitors. As we took seats in the grandstand and waited, we too began to wonder when the bus would arrive for it was nearly time for the junior varsity game to begin. Finally, much to our relief we spotted Vinnie, Jimmy, and the remaining players trooping in. However, the usual gaggle of cheerleaders and students didn't follow.

I rushed over to Vinnie and asked, "Where is everybody?" "Oh, the bus broke down so we had to come in cars." Jimmy asked, "How the hell did you guys get here?"

"Oh, my God," I immediately thought. "How are we going to get home?" I could see Peewee's mind working overtime so I quickly said, "If you're thinking of hitch-hiking back, forget it! I'm not going to freeze to death out there."

Turned out the team was able to commandeer only three cars to transport them, and a few of the junior varsity players had to be left behind. The coach spotted me and spoke to his manager. "Want to play?" Jimmy inquired. He didn't have to ask twice as I rushed over to the locker room and got into uniform. I always wore my basketball sneakers and was used to playing in street clothes at the Boys Club, so not having all the usual paraphernalia, such as a jock strap and a towel to shower with, wouldn't be a problem.

Being pressed into service as a team member took my mind off our transportation predicament—for a little while. Vinnie sat on the bench next to the coach during the junior varsity game and offered me encouragement and advice. "Remember what I told you," he said, and I racked my brain to dredge up the particular instruction to which he referred. I got to play sparingly but scored three points. Vinnie, as usual, was his dazzling self in the varsity game, leading our team to a resounding victory.

When it was all over, I followed the referees, one of whom lived up the street from me, and asked if we could catch a ride home with him. The ref teasingly said, "Need a ride 'eh?" and after a long pause added, "Yeah, you can come with us." Even Peewee breathed a sigh of relief, and we eagerly jumped into the backseat of his car. As we left the parking lot, I became puzzled as to why the car had turned north instead of south, from whence we had come. The reason soon became apparent when the ref pulled up in front of the town's lone bar and grill. We had no choice but to follow the two men into the tavern. The place reeked of stale beer, and the tables were populated with rough-looking lumberjacks swilling foamy brews.

Adding to our surprise, a few minutes later Vinnie and Jimmy and the rest of our team also entered the bar. The coach, who reputedly enjoyed bending an elbow now and again, apparently wasn't a stickler about his boys also having a drink or two.

Everyone bellied up to the long bar except Peewee, who didn't have a chance of passing the eighteen-year-old drinking age test. I found a spot between Vinnie and Jimmy, and tried to put on what I thought was an "I'm old-enough-to-drink face." The bartender looked at me indifferently and asked, "What'll you have?" "A draft," I replied rather spontaneously, surprising Vinnie who looked over and with his penetrating blue eyes said through a smile, "That'll put hair on your chest." It was the first beer I'd ever had, and after I sipped the last drop of the foaming liquid, the bartender set up another without even asking. I drank the second much more slowly and when I finally finished, my thoughts were doing laps around my brain cells. Vinnie said, "I think that's enough kiddo, or I'll be picking you up off the floor."

The refs downed their final quaffs, and we were soon on the road back to Carthage. When I arrived home I was greeted with an alarm-tinged, "Where have you been?" from my mom who had been nervously awaiting my return. Apparently the news of the bus mishap had traveled around the village, finally reaching mom's ears. I confessed to the hitch-hiking caper, leaving out of course, the part about drinking beer. Mom was in a surprisingly forgiving mood, and I was sent off to bed without further reprimand.

After Vinnie's graduation the following June, he

was drafted into the Army, just a few months before the war ended. He did a stint in the Far East as a military policeman and was discharged when two years of service were up. He took a stab at college when he returned, but stayed only one semester and again came home. I was now in my senior year at Augustinian, and although I wondered about it I never knew, and Vinnie never said, why college didn't work out for him. He certainly was smart enough but apparently there were things bothering him about which he never spoke. Jimmy and I both noticed that Vinnie had changed from his former carefree self to one who was more reserved and calculating when he spoke.

Jobs were scarce back then, primarily due to the glut of returning veterans, so Vinnie took to hanging around the Boys Club and Jimmy's store. He played basketball with the younger kids and passed the time in conversation while puzzling over what he was going to do with the rest of his life. I visited the grocery periodically to engage Jimmy and Vinnie in conversation, which I enjoyed immensely, because they treated me as an intellectual equal.

World affairs and the coming presidential election were but a couple of the subjects that we hotly discussed. One day, during one of our debates, Vinnie announced that he had studied all the candidates and was casting his vote for Henry Agard Wallace, the former vice president under Roosevelt some four years before. While still in office back in 1944, Wallace was dumped from the presidential ticket in favor of Harry S Truman. The Democratic kingmakers were certain that Roosevelt wouldn't last out his term, and they were loath to have a perceived Communist sympathizer become president. Of course, Roosevelt did die in office and Truman succeeded him in 1945. After the war was over, Wallace took to severely criticizing Truman's foreign policy and subsequently decided to run against him as a third party candidate in the election of '48.

One concern that Vinnie often brought up was that it took only three years to completely dissipate all the good will the Russians had built up as America's ally during the war. Of course we all knew about the Iron Curtain slamming down across Eastern Europe— verifying that Communism was an evil system. To be called a "sympathizer," which had become a fashionable media slur, was the kiss of death for any politician, certainly one running for president. That's why Vinnie's pronouncement of support for Wallace shocked both Jimmy and me, because we knew *he* was one of *those*. But the more we discussed it, the more passionate Vinnie became and it greatly perplexed me.

One day, while Vinnie was waxing eloquently about Wallace, it suddenly occurred to me that if he were really sincere about his convictions he should try to proselytize a complete stranger. "Why don't you convince the next person who comes into the store to vote for Wallace?" I suggested, half in jest. Vinnie pondered this idea for a few moments and then accepted the challenge.

Almost immediately the door opened and in strolled the Wonder Bread deliveryman. Vinnie waited until the breadman had stacked the shelves, written out the bill, and was settling up with Jimmy before sidling up to him to begin his pitch. "Excuse me, sir," he began, "have you considered giving Henry Wallace your vote for president in the coming election?" Completely taken aback, the man smiled nervously and looked askance as Vinnie quickly and somewhat nervously ran through a checklist of his candidate's accomplishments. Finally, having settled up with Jimmy and looking a bit beleaguered, the breadman said, "Well, that's all very interesting, young man. I'll certainly take it into consideration." With that, he quickly made his escape out the door.

Neither Jimmy nor I could contain our laughter— not because we thought Vinnie had made a fool of himself—but because, although we admired the courage of his convictions, the surrealistic scene that unfolded was truly comical. The reaction of the startled deliveryman to Vinnie's pleadings, a cause to which neither of us subscribed, was humorous and impressive, all at the same time.

As we would soon discover, Vinnie had other surprises in store for us. Not only were his political convictions out in left field, but so too were his religious beliefs. I had thought, mainly because of the strict parochial education we both had been subjected to at Augustinian, that there wasn't any room for discussion of the chiseled-in-stone tenets we were taught. I therefore became increasingly uneasy whenever Vinnie brought up the subject of religion. He had become disenchanted with the Church and had stopped attending altogether. Now as a man of the world, he'd begun to question just about everything, even the existence of God. "Jeez," I thought. "Vinnie's not only a Communist sympathizer but an agnostic, or worse, an atheist!"

Surprise, however, turned to shock when Vinnie announced one day that he had joined the Marine Corps. He'd decided to see more of the world and re-entering military service would provide that opportunity. After he left for Quantico, Jimmy and I continued our periodic discussions while lamenting the loss of Vinnie's companionship. We often wondered aloud how he was doing down at Parris Island but neither of us heard from him.

Three weeks after Vinnie left, I popped in to see Jimmy and saw he was totally engrossed in the afternoon newspaper. He didn't even look up when I came in, as he usually did. Finally, he slowly raised his head and said, . . . "Vinnie's dead!"

"What?" I was so shocked that my vocabulary totally failed me. "The papers are calling it an 'accident,'" Jimmy said, "but it's couched in a peculiar way. It happened in the barracks, one evening a few days ago. They said he was cleaning his rifle."

I could see Jimmy had a lump in his throat as he spoke, and that he doubted the truth of the paper's story. After I left the store, walking up the street alone, I began to cry. I couldn't understand why a bright, talented young man like Vinnie, a guy I loved as a brother and wanted so much to be like, could lose his life in such a senseless way.

The next day I visited Jimmy again and he told me that he'd heard from someone close to the family that Vinnie had put his rifle under his chin . . . and fired. This only brought tears anew, now in front of Jimmy. "How could he take his own life?" I sobbed. Jimmy, as disconsolate as I, said he didn't know.

Jimmy and I sat in the back of the church while attending Vinnie's funeral. We didn't want to intrude on the family, whom we knew were not only greatly aggrieved over the loss of a family member, but also agonizing silently over the circumstances of his death.

We both couldn't help but wonder if Vinnie would have approved of the ceremony that gave him his final sendoff.

Strickland Bulding

5

Some of the jobs I held during my high school years, besides peddling the *Syracuse Post Standard* in the morning and the *Watertown Daily Times* in the afternoon, involved working in a couple of the town's grocery stores. In addition to the A&P there were two other chain stores, Market Basket and Grand Union. I stocked shelves at the former and worked behind the meat counter at the latter. The Market Basket was located in the Strickland Building, the same business block as pop's store, and was where I first really got to understand the social pecking order of the smaller-minded people of our little town.

The store manager, whom I thought was a friend of my dad's, gave me a stocker's job at the wage of thirty five cents an hour. He kept me busy, not only stocking shelves, but also helping unload the delivery truck that came once a week. The hundred-pound sacks of potatoes were heavy, but I dutifully toted them from the truck to the stockroom. I also boxed groceries at the checkout counter. I say boxed because we recycled the cardboard boxes that canned goods came in instead of using paper bags, whenever possible. The manager felt it was his duty

Academy Basketball Team, 1948 – 49

to see that I was never idle, so he was always after me to do something.

What bothered me no end was the discovery that Bob, another boy who worked there and whose dad was an insurance salesman, told me he was getting fifty cents an hour! Since the labor was the same, I couldn't understand why he was worth nearly fifty percent more. I also noticed that the manager was much easier on Bob and didn't boss him around the same way he did me. It finally dawned on me that the only difference between us was that I was from the lower class, darker immigrant group.

The next time Adam Lofink, the owner of the Ford garage, was in the store, I casually asked if he needed any help. "Sure," he said. "Come by on Monday and I'll give you a job." I abruptly quit the Market Basket and went to the Ford garage for a raise to fifty cents per hour. I learned how to grease cars and pump gas and liked the mechanics I worked around, all of whom were willing to teach me the ropes.

There was an incident at the garage shortly after I left. The grease rack, which I spent many an hour under, suddenly collapsed one day. Luckily the mechanic had stepped out from under to wipe off his grease gun when the hoist, along with an automobile, came crashing down. There was no safety mechanism on the rack. I shuddered when I heard about what happened.

I quite accidentally met up with Market Basket Bob fifteen years later while working at General Electric. We had a short chat, and I could see the disappointment on his face when he discovered I was three levels higher than he and had already made supervisor's rank. GE didn't

Pop's Store, 1943

seem to care that he was from my hometown's upper class. Nonetheless, his dad used to come into pop's store to brag about how well his son Bob was doing at General Electric. "Big job, big job," he'd exclaim. I had to chuckle when my dad reported that to me. Status is important in small towns.

After graduating from high school, I continued working in pop's store whenever I couldn't find employment anywhere else. As I mentioned before, jobs were hard to come by and most of my friends were entering military service as one of their better employment options.

Carthage had a full-time, handsome Air Force recruiter who was not only a very persuasive guy, but cut a dashing figure in his medal-studded uniform. Recent high school grads were squarely in his bombsights, and I was one of them. He came into pop's store often and once suggested I take the enlistment exams. I decided to take up the offer, mainly because most of my friends were, and I was curious as to how I'd score. The exams were fairly elementary, and I did so well that the recruiter made a point of talking to my mom about me joining up. He told her he wanted me "more than any other kid in the county." Although my mom was flattered, I knew it was just a sales pitch and had my mind set on going back to Augustinian for a post graduate year. The opportunity to play another year of basketball was irresistible, and our coach, Howard Splete, who was also the Boys Club director, told me I could have my dream job as gym supervisor if I came back. That was icing on the cake as I'd only recently turned seventeen and would have needed parental consent to enlist anyway, a permission that I didn't intend to ask for.

The recruiter didn't give up easily. He owned a small plane that was parked at a converted cow pasture that served as the local airfield. All boys my age were enamored with flying and most of us could name all the WWII aces and their planes. Thinking that I scored well enough to qualify for pilot training, the recruiter asked if I'd like to go for ride in his plane. "Great," I said. So, at the appointed time I eagerly jumped into his car for the trip to the airfield. This would be my very first plane ride, and I was quite excited. Things went great at first but then my pilot decided to show me some maneuvers like figure eights, loops, and barrel rolls. My stomach decided to do similar maneuvers on its own, and when the pilot saw me turning green, he made a quick landing. I got sick as the proverbial dog, and promptly threw up my flying career.

In my post-graduate year I was named captain of the basketball team, and also pitched for the baseball nine. To tell the truth, I hated to leave school, despite nuns like Sister Camilla, because it had become such a large and enjoyable part of my life. I was taking just three subjects at school, playing basketball four hours a day, supervising the Boys Club gym, and working in my dad's store. It turned out to be a more exciting year than I thought as you will see from the following tale.

Pop's Store

SEVEN DAYS A WEEK, THREE HUNDRED sixty five days a year—that was pop's routine for most of his working life. His small cigar store on Mechanic Street in Carthage was opened at seven in the morning and closed at eleven at night. His core business consisted of traditional tobacco products, magazines and newspapers. But because of his ingrained Lebanese peddler instincts, he was always on the lookout for new products to sell. Over the years he added such items as ice cream, ballpoint pens, antacid pills, aspirin, books for rent, and even condoms—which were secreted in a compartment inside the tall cigarette display case. The latter item was for his regular customers who were too bashful to ask for them at the local pharmacy. This was in a long since forgotten puritanical era, before such items were freely placed on drugstore shelves. It wasn't the only secret compartment that my dad had in the store, as another housed a Colt .32 special pistol. No one was going to rob pop of his hard-earned nickels and dimes, not without a fight at any rate.

After World War II ended and public morals began to relax somewhat, gambling began to proliferate and pop decided this could also be a lucrative source of revenue. He soon came to offer football pools, nickel and dime chances on a punchboard, and lottery tickets, all of which were illegal of course. The local authorities, however, winked at these activities—why, even the police chief's wife regularly bought lottery tickets.

An organized crime syndicate out of Utica, New York ran the popular lottery numbers racket, along with the football parleys. The lottery tickets contained numbers that used the last five digits of the daily US Treasury balance. Purchasers could consult their newspapers to see if their numbers matched. What the syndicate didn't take into account, however, was the simmering political situation that existed in the summer of 1948. Former district attorney, incumbent

New York State Governor, and Republican presidential candidate Thomas E. Dewey was seeking ways to embellish his already substantial reputation for being tough on crime.

This was also the summer pop was incapacitated due to a gall bladder operation, and one week after high school graduation I was placed in total charge of the store. Proud to have been entrusted by pop to handle it all by myself, I was really enjoying being the boss. I even carried the same large wad of bills in my pocket that my dad did.

A couple of weeks later, on a bright and sunny Saturday morning in July, I noticed a state trooper's car pull up and park in front of the store. Although cops and troopers often frequented the store, and pop was on a first name basis with many of them, it seemed curious only because the two officers just sat in their cruiser, staring into the store. I soon came to understand why. Promptly at 10:00 AM, they emerged from their patrol car and entered the store. The tall, muscular troopers swaggered in with their leather belts and boots creaking with every intimidating step. The sergeant in charge approached the counter, while the second stood back with one hand resting lazily on his holstered revolver.

The lead trooper quickly announced their mission. "We've come for the lottery tickets!" After recovering from this shocking proclamation, I regained enough composure to feign ignorance of any lottery tickets. "I have no idea what you're talking about," I sputtered.

My denial fell on deaf ears, of course, and the officer said, "Look kid, we can do this the easy way or the hard way. It's your choice. You can give them up or I can start looking for them." With that threat, the trooper showed me what he said was a search warrant.

The menacing urgency of the trooper's voice threw me into a panic for I thought I was going to be arrested and would have a criminal record for the rest of my life. I quickly reached under the counter for the cigar box that held the contraband. There were many more tickets hidden in a different compartment but since the lawman didn't ask, I decided not to volunteer them.

You see, pop's store was also a drop off point for tickets that would be picked up by one of the mob's couriers and taken further north to sellers in Star Lake and beyond, all the way up to the Canadian border. I was a bit surprised that John Law didn't know about this arrangement.

So, after handing me a subpoena to appear before a grand jury in Syracuse two months hence, they left to pay a visit on my recuperating father at home. When the bathrobed convalescent descended the creaky stairs, his first thought was the lawmen were paying him a courtesy call. But his usual congenial manner quickly faded when one of the troopers handed him a similar subpoena for the same grand jury. At least they didn't ask him to cough up any tickets.

The incident soon became the talk of the town, as newspapers across the state played up the story of Governor Dewey's smashing the extensive gambling ring. Try as I might to be excused from appearing at the grand jury, even writing a letter to the district attorney claiming that I was joining the armed forces with several of my friends, which by the way, I really had no intention of doing, I was not to be excused. Thus in September, my dad and I boarded a bus to Syracuse, some ninety miles away, to appear before the convened grand jury.

I waited anxiously in an anteroom while my father went in to testify. He was in and out in less than five minutes. I was summoned next. The courtroom was intimidating, large, and I couldn't help but notice the impressive woodwork, the carved arches, railings, and paneled walls. In addition to the judge and twelve impaneled jurors, there was a substantial gallery packed with spectators.

"Raise your right hand," the burly bailiff barked before proceeding to administer the oath. After being duly sworn, I was confronted by the dapper DA, who was running a comb through his hair while sauntering over to the witness box to begin his questioning. He was of medium height and wore an expensive suit under his now neatly coifed brown, wavy hair. This was a man obviously on his way up the political ladder, one who knew how to play up to the half-dozen or so newsmen and flash-bulb popping photographers seated in the front row.

The prosecutor decided to have some fun with me, I think to liven up his audience. His first query concerned my trying to get out of appearing in front of his grand jury. "You didn't want to come visit us?" he asked with a saccharine smile. "Going into the service, eh?" He brushed aside my attempts to explain and continued with more lighthearted repartee by asking me my age and what grade I was in at school. I replied that I was seventeen and had graduated high school the previous June. He smiled broadly and said, "Kind of backward aren't you?" to the laughter-punctuated amusement of his audience.

After what seemed to be an eternity of this style of banter, he suddenly changed gears, went to the evidence table directly in front of the judge and picked up what

I soon realized was a felon's mug shot—with front and side views and a string of numbers below. He stuck it in my face and gravely asked, "Do you recognize this man?"

It was the guy who used to bring the lottery tickets to my dad's store. "Sure," I quickly said, wanting to be cooperative, "that's Sam Ross."

Sam was a large, suave, ruddy-faced guy of about sixty who dressed in custom tailored suits, wore a fine felt fedora over his neatly combed gray hair, and always had a long, fat cigar clenched between his teeth. His nose, which prominently protruded from his ruddy face, was a bit bulbous and probably the result of enjoying too many scotch and sodas. When Sam came by to pick up the proceeds and pay off the winning tickets, which by the way were few and far between, he arrived in a long white Cadillac that I greatly admired. One time he even suggested that I get myself a cheap car, a "flivver" he called it, and he'd give me my own route to peddle lottery tickets. I was really attracted to the proposition, but my dad wasn't, and that idea was quickly given the door.

"Sam Ross!" the DA bellowed. "Don't you know this man to be Samuel Rosencrantz?"

"Oh, no," I said. "That's Sam Ross."

The DA wasn't happy with my proclamation as he apparently didn't know Ross's alias just as I didn't know his true name was Rosencrantz. What had been a fairly amiable and humorous session, despite my nervousness, suddenly turned very serious. He pivoted, walked over to the evidence table and in a Perry Mason like move, grabbed one of the notorious lottery tickets, wheeled and fanned it in front of me.

"Does this look like the ticket you sold to Sergeant

Hamilton of the Bureau of Criminal Investigation?" he demanded with a self-satisfied smirk. I knew I had never sold tickets to people I didn't know, certainly not a cop, so I peered carefully at the specimen and finally said, "I don't know sir, they all look alike, don't they?" At that point my antagonist shouted, *"I repeat, does this look like the ticket you sold to Sergeant Hamilton of the BCI?"*

I suddenly had visions of being cuffed and frog-marched off to the nearest lockup, so I quickly responded, "Yes sir. That's the one, for sure that's the one."

When I finally exited the jury room, my dad asked what I had been doing in there for twenty minutes. The DA, who had followed me out, and in what I felt was a let-bygones-be-bygones gesture, put his arm around my shoulders and said to my dad, "You have a fine boy here, Mr Ellis." My dad smiled and nodded, relieved that this ordeal was over, even though he had lost a fairly good source of revenue.

In any event, the lottery ticket furor soon died down, and when the presidential election was held a couple of months later, Thomas E. Dewey, the crusading, crime-busting, odds-on favorite . . . lost.

St. James Church

6

I'LL BE THE FIRST TO ADMIT THAT I WAS AN aimless lad after finally and reluctantly exiting high school. My dad asked what I was going to do now that my schooling was finished. "How about I become a partner in the store?" I naively asked. "No," pop replied. "This is a one-man business. You'll have to find your own way." "Maybe I should go to college," I offered. "How much money do you have in the bank?" he asked. "I've got $600," I proudly answered. This represented the princely sum I had saved by working all those different jobs, while miserly denying myself many of the simplest pleasures that other youth indulged in. "Well," he said, "take your money and go. When you get your report card, bring it home and if it looks like you're going to make something of yourself, maybe I'll help you."

Long story short, my initial stabs at college were unsuccessful. I wasn't ready for that phase of my life so I returned home and took a succession of jobs that included milkman and paper mill hand. In retrospect, all my work experiences were useful to me later in life, if for nothing more than to appreciate what most people go through to eke out a living. It also gave me a greater impetus to try to improve my life through higher education. Using my brains instead of my back became much more appealing to me.

That fall I sat for the International Association of Approved Basketball Officials (IAABO) exam so that I might continue my association with the sport that I loved. The exam consisted of fifty questions and I tied another older guy for the high score of ninety-six on the test, missing on just two answers. I was eighteen at the time and, as the lowest ranking official, was assigned mostly junior varsity games. If a scheduling conflict arose, or an official was indisposed, I would occasionally get to do a varsity game as well. I knew the rules front to back, of course, and was a stickler for their enforcement. I once took away a foul shot from a player for taking longer than ten seconds to get it off. No one seemed to know this rule existed. My reputation for enforcement soon led to one very memorable experience.

I was assigned a varsity game at Theresa High School along with Luke Diamond, a veteran official who had refereed many Syracuse University games. Unfortunately, the Theresa team woefully outclassed its opponent from Chaumont, New York. The game was a runaway before the half ended and the Chaumont coach became extremely lathered up. He decided to take his frustration out on the junior member of the officiating team, namely me.

As I was trotting by the visitor's bench I heard the coach tell one of his players, "Get in there and kill him!" "Whoa," I thought, "what kind of coaching is that?" On the very next play, I ejected that player for an egregious foul. The coach sent in another player with the same instruction. Another ejection soon followed. The Chaumont team lost by some thirty points.

After the game, the coach came into the ref's room to tell me that he had just witnessed the worst refereed game of his life and his principal agreed with him. He parted with, "You've got a game scheduled with us at home in two months. Don't bother to show up. You won't be allowed in the building!" I said, "That's fine with me. Just send me the check. I've been assigned the game, and I expect to get paid for it."

I was disappointed that Luke didn't stand up for me. After the coach left he said, "There was no call for that at all."

A couple of weeks later I got a hand-written note from the aggrieved coach in which he claimed he had been under a lot of stress and profusely apologized for his behavior. He added that the principal hadn't agreed with him as he had claimed. "You will be welcomed in Chaumont for our game next month." I did go and couldn't have been treated more cordially. Chaumont lost again by more than thirty points.

In June 1950, while working with an Italian marble artisan who was installing a new altar at St James Church, the news broke about North Korea invading the South. I was flabbergasted. The last war had been over only five years. What was the world coming to? I remember thinking that a decent interval would be something approaching twenty years, the span between WWI and WWII.

The invasion set off a mad scramble to get our armed forces, which had fallen into disrepair, up to speed. Soon draft notices and calls to reservists hit post offices across the country. There was no patriotic scramble to join, as there was at the onset of WWII. Most boys, myself included, didn't see rushing off to Korea as somehow defending our freedoms. To avoid the call-up, many began joining the National Guard and US Army Reserves. Camp Drum, formerly Pine Camp, is only eight miles from Carthage and was where many reserve units were based. Recruiters came out of the woodwork, telling boys they could serve their time at home—an attractive proposition to many.

I resisted even this opportunity at first but finally succumbed to the lure and joined the 314th Military Police detachment. I dutifully went to meetings once a week and spent two weeks in the summer running around the Pine Plains in military regalia. The Draft Board was still after me nonetheless, and when my number came up, I was summoned to take a physical in Syracuse. About the same time, our government announced that the new GI Bill had passed Congress. This was a game changer for me as I now saw service as a way to pay for my college education. Shortly thereafter, I volunteered for a two year stint of active duty.

The war in Korea was raging and boys were being killed. I was lucky however, as I got assigned to the Adjutant General branch and would eventually become a glorified clerk—acquiring the fancy title of Administrative NCO.

From my perspective, service in the Army turned out to be a great experience. It finally forced me out of my home environment and into the variegated world of different races, ethnicities, cultures, and educational backgrounds. The Army, in spite of all its inefficiencies, forced young men to cohabit and get along with each other. My eyes were opened to a whole new world and it was just what I needed to jump-start my life away from Carthage, New York.

The following story encapsulates some of my experiences and observations during my active service.

You're in the Army Now

NOT LONG AFTER MY ORDERS TO REPORT for induction arrived, I was at the railroad station, boarding a coach that would start me on my journey to Fort Dix, New Jersey. As the 11:00 PM train to New York City chugged away from the station, I grew increasingly apprehensive. I glanced around the coach at my fellow passengers and wondered if any of them were also reporting for duty, but nothing in their behavior or baggage betrayed their business.

I gazed out the window to see the place where I had lived all my life quickly fading to black. Peering into the darkness, I began to feel terribly alone and homesick. My emotions were betraying me, even though I had audaciously told everyone I was eager to leave home and embark on new adventures. My mother had worried aloud to her friends about my leaving her sheltering eyes, and this embarrassed me no end. I told myself that I was glad to be out from under Mama's incessant gaze, even if it meant venturing into the unknown world of war. Lebanese mothers, it seems to me, are overly protective of their sons, and I didn't like it at all. This had been but one of many factors in my desire to shed my ethnic identity. I fervently believed in the melting pot ideal of America taught at school and desired nothing more than to blend in with

In The Army Now

my peer group, to become accepted as a true American.

The first leg of my journey would take nine hours, yet despite the lateness of the hour and the rhythmic clack-clack of the train's wheels I was not lulled to sleep. As the clock hands crept past 1:00 AM, I was still wide-awake and would remain so the whole night. At eight in the morning the train pulled into Grand Central Station. I was a bit bleary-eyed as I entered the main concourse, and found my way to the shuttle for Penn Station where I boarded another train to Trenton. From there I hopped on a bus that took me and a gaggle of other boys to Fort Dix.

As I stood in the reservists' line for my physical, I became alarmed by the routine acceptance of many seemingly unfit specimens for duty. One lad with thick glasses was so pigeon-toed he couldn't walk without placing one foot directly in the path of the other. Selective Service Boards from around the nation were heroically meeting their quotas by scouring barrel bottoms all across the nation. The conscription rolls for this so-called police action had even tagged men who were classified 4-F (physically unable to perform) in the last war. Others who had served in WWII, and didn't realize they had been kept in reserve status, were also being called back. To me, an athletically fit ballplayer, this assemblage of humanity did little to augment my confidence in the country's ability to successfully wage war. If these boys truly represented the flower of American manhood, the bouquet had been seriously infested with weeds. It was stark testimony, either to the urgency of this war, or the scarcity of men to fight it.

I soon realized that my barracks housed a group of men that had come not only from all walks of life but also every social stratum. There were urban blacks and Latinos, along with farm boys from rural America, and a smattering of recent college graduates whose deferments had run out. Education levels ranged from eighth-grade dropouts to graduate degrees, and previous occupations ran the gamut from common laborers to a variety of professionals—as well as a smattering of common criminals—from the cream of the crop to the dregs of society. I hadn't known any Puerto Ricans or black men before, but in the Army there was a disproportionate number of both. War seemed to favor minorities in an unfavorable way. Never, it seems, is the mosaic of American manhood more diversely congregated than in times of national need.

I didn't spot any Lebanese boys in my group, at least not by facial features, and I wasn't sure why this even crossed my mind. Perhaps I had an innate desire to avoid the personal recognition that would follow. I wasn't sure.

Service in Uncle Sam's Army presented unanticipated educational opportunities. The first of the primary directives I would master was: "Do not trust your fellow man!" Street-wise kids from New York City seemed to lay in wait for rubes like me. They borrowed money with sob stories, money that would never be returned. They got suckers to cover work details for them, or to take the rap for their goldbricking, while also cheating them at cards. It would take awhile but my smiling and friendly countenance would eventually turn into a frowning and wary one. I would become very choosy about the friends I made.

"Where you from, Ellis?" I was asked. Nobody had ever heard of Carthage, or really cared where it was. But it was a question, along with "What are you? English? You don't look English. You look more like a Greek." Those were but a few of the comments and questions that I was asked in the first few weeks of service. "I'm American!" I would answer, and I couldn't quite pinpoint why I felt a twinge of guilt about this response. I recalled that my father gave that same response when registering me at the hospital to get my tonsils removed. pop had said, "We're American," to the startled receptionist who had asked our nationality. Although only ten at the time, I never forgot my obvious surprise, and when my expression betrayed me, my father turned and said, "Well, we're citizens, aren't we?"

Eating in the army mess hall continually provided new culinary experiences for me. I never got used to a breakfast of creamed beef on toast, which is known to Army men as SOS (shit on a shingle in Army vernacular)—not something you want to be thinking about when eating your first meal of the day. I looked forward to having Salisbury steak when I saw it on the menu. It turned out to be just a fancy name for hamburger. Truthfully I would have much preferred *kibbe,* a staple of my diet growing up. There were lots of strange foods I had to consume, or go hungry. Nothing on the menu resembled what my mother regularly cooked at home.

I soon learned that if I was going to blend in and become one of the boys I would have to make significant modifications to the Queen's English that I had brought with me. The argot of the Army's everyday common communication required me to seek a much lower common denominator. This was due to the omnipresent compound word "motherfucker" that was a required epithet in every conversation.

Now it wasn't that I had never heard that particular coinage before. After all I wasn't delivered to Fort Dix on the back of a cabbage truck. It was the frequency, rapidity, and universality of its usage that shocked me. I guess you could say I was a bit shy and hesitant to take up this clarion call because my religious mother never tolerated bad language in her presence—certainly not in English. When my pop became unduly exasperated, he always resorted to his native Arabic to express his anger. Consequently I learned a rather extensive litany of Lebanese imprecations, although I didn't know the exact meaning of most of them.

My comrades in arms, however, were not hesitant to comply with the Army's *lingua franca*, even if they did so apprehensively at first. As time wore on, trepidation wore off and nearly everyone embraced this particular epithet with uncommon devotion.

It was amazing that such a relatively recent, albeit dubious invective, could be delivered with such variety, emotion, and gusto. The Puerto Ricans would ejaculate these fulminations through clenched teeth, like a thrown stiletto. Many Blacks abbreviated the word into an economical "mofo." Further adding to its enrichment were the different dialects that decorated its pronunciation, which ran the gamut from Brooklynese to Alabaman drawl. But, with the passage of time, everyone embraced this particular appellation as a necessary part of their vocabulary.

It amazed me that such a noxious execration could be delivered with such variety, verve, and enthusiasm. At times "motherfucker" was a noun, verb, adjective, adverb, or gerund—even in the same tortured sentence. The count was staggering. And, the damn word wasn't even in the dictionary!

Probably the second most commonly used verbal construct in the Army was "goddamn." God damned just about everything in sight and did so with alarming regularity. Although armies traveled on their stomachs as Napoleon had sagely said, I don't think even he foresaw that this man's Army would march forth on a bellyful of motherfucks and goddamns. And a pretty rapid cadence it was, one that nearly every GI struggled to keep pace with. The well-bred college graduates from the privileged class, who delivered their motherfucks and goddamns a bit tentatively at first, soon assumed the vigor and assurance of the underclass as their usage increased. Once a soldier had completed his basic training, his verbal skills, such as they might have been at the outset, would have been completely dumbed down to accommodate the language of his environment.

It wasn't long before I no longer took notice of these ubiquitous expressions as they became so commonplace that they lost all their attention-getting properties. No more shock, no more embarrassment. What passed as normal conversation in the Army was considered lewd and lascivious everywhere else.

I had always aspired to a college education and intended to fulfill that dream when my hitch was up. The GI Bill, I believed, would be my ticket into the upper class. After prolonged scrutiny of my better-educated comrades, I became disappointed as I saw these collegiate products fall short of my expectations. I had been conditioned to consider educated people and anyone with a white-collar job as someone to be looked up to. I often heard Lebanese women say admiringly of their sons, "He works in an office," the meaning of which was obvious. The list of esteemed workers also encompassed anyone who didn't make his living by getting his hands dirty. Officers in the military were, of course, also included in this elevated class.

Because of this conditioning I necessarily viewed officers as smarter than enlisted types—men to look up to. It soon became apparent that, in the wisdom of running wars and choosing the leadership attendant thereto, Uncle Sam was less than perfect. The officers, as well as enlisted men, came from the nooks and crannies of the civilian cupboard. Uncle's margin of error seemed to be especially large in times of desperate conscription, and stunted language skills were not the sole province of the lower ranks.

One day, while preparing for a training exercise in reconnoitering, the company commander, who rumor had it came to active duty from an auto body shop in the Midwest, was readying us for a march with his final instructions. We would all have to converge on the same god-forsaken piece of real estate in an adjacent god-forsaken swamp, at nearly the same moment in time. "All right men," he bellowed as he checked his timepiece. "It's precisely oh-seven-two-oh, let's *simonize* our watches."

One of the college educated men in my barracks was a shy, introverted Harvard grad from Boston by the name of Howard Broberg. He reportedly had a genius IQ and his Ivy League speech, rationed to begin with, did not allow for the incorporation of the crudities of his bunkmates. He had once been overheard, in a rare conversation, mentioning to one of the men that he and his brother collected Duesenberg cars. "Yeah, sure, the motherfucker collects antique cars," Leroy said and everybody had a good laugh at Howard's expense. His comrades soon took to calling him "Doozey," even those who had never before heard of that brand of automobile or knew what that expression meant. "It's a Doozey," was derived from the reputed excellence of the Duesenberg automobile. You could see that Howard's feelings were hurt, not only because he was now the butt of jokes by his bunkmates, but was also labeled a liar. Collecting antique cars indeed! It almost made him want to cuss.

One Monday morning a few weeks later, while we were lined up for roll call, it soon became apparent that Doozey was absent. "Maybe the motherfucker finally cracked up and went over the hill," said Leroy.

As was often done, I decided to risk answering "here" for Howard when his name came up in the hope that he would show before we had to report for duty. Just as roll call began, a roar was heard in the distance, getting increasingly louder as it came towards our barracks. We all looked out in the direction of the clamor and could see a column of black smoke heading in our direction.

"What the hell is that motherfucking racket?" our Sergeant shouted. Soon, a dilapidated, blue, 1928, Model A Duesenberg—obviously needing a muffler among other niceties it had sported in better times— roared into the parking lot. Out stepped Howard with the look of a nerd who had just shown up at the senior prom with the homecoming queen. "Check out this motherfucking, goddamned Doozey!" he shouted. We couldn't believe our eyes. Howard had killed two birds with the same stone.

The first time I became eligible for a weekend pass, I decided to go to New York City to take in the sights and perhaps catch a ballgame by my favorite team, the Giants. When I arrived, alone and hungry, my first instinct was to look in the Yellow Pages for, of all things, a Middle Eastern restaurant. I found a place on 32nd Street called Damascus Gardens and made my way to the second floor eatery. Inhaling the familiar odors as I climbed the stairs, I was directed to a table where I was seated and given a menu. I ordered a large plate of stuffed grape leaves, along with yogurt, hummus, and copious amounts of flat mountain bread. As I consumed these delicacies my mind was awash with childhood memories, and I had to forcibly suppress a tear that threatened to spill down my cheek. I didn't understand this conflict of emotions. Was it the pleasant sensations of the longed-for food or the embarrassment I felt for consciously shunning my ethnicity?

By the time my hitch was up two years later, although I was still wary of making friends, I'd tell anyone who asked what kind of name Ellis was—"it's Lebanese!" Thanks to you, Uncle Sam, I had come back home.

7

WHEN MY SERVICE OBLIGATION neared its end, I applied and was admitted to LeMoyne College in Syracuse. Loretta, my girlfriend of four and a half years, and I decided to get married a week before I mustered out of the service, thereby getting to spend our honeymoon in New York City while my discharge was completed at Ft. Hamilton.

College would be hectically compressed into three years because I was now in a great hurry to get a degree and start earning some real money. I got a part-time job, logging thirty hours a week at the Syracuse Tuberculosis Clinic taking chest x-rays, which greatly supplemented my $120 per month GI Bill benefit. My wife, Loretta, also worked at the Veterans Administration until our first child was born two years later. Our $18 per month apartment was a second floor cold water flat that was still under rent control. A few pieces of cheap furniture, some linoleum for the floors, and we settled in for the duration.

I have often admitted to myself that because of my schedule of classes (up to twenty-one hours per week), I missed out on the usual college experiences that alumni

Graduation, LeMoyne College

fondly dredge up at reunions. I went to summer school three years in a row, spent one night a week at Army Reserve meetings, including two weeks of Reserve duty at summer camp, and between school, the job, and studying, had no time left over. There were no parties, beer busts, bar hopping, or dances for me because I was in a hurry to make up for lost time. In retrospect, I regret that I didn't take more time to savor the experience.

As my third and final year was coming to a close, I began applying for jobs. The largest employer in the area was General Electric, and I dutifully sent in an application. No response. One day when I was at my dentist's, he asked what I was going to do now that college was nearly over. I told him I was looking and about my sad experience with GE. He offered that one of his neighbors was a "big wheel" with the company, and would I like him to make an inquiry on my behalf? Would I! The following week I got a call from a GE personnel man and he asked me to send in an application. "Already did," I said. "Can't find it," he said. "Send another."

A week later I was sitting in the foyer of the very secret Heavy Military Electronics Equipment Department, waiting to be interviewed. The man who came out looked me over and asked, "So, what experience do you bring to us?" I replied that I was sure I had none that was applicable to what he was doing but I had brought along a transcript of my grades. After looking it over, and inquiring as to what texts we used for this or that subject, he asked, "Well, what would you like to do?" "Work," I emphatically replied. He smiled and asked, "When would you like to start?" "Well, my last exam is on Friday. How about Monday?" "Good, report here

Monday morning."

That's how my ten year career with GE started. It has often made me wonder how life changing events turn on some of the smallest incidents. Suppose I'd had a different dentist? Or suppose my appointment had been a few months later? Life is funny that way.

GE was where I first encountered computers. I'd never seen one before and didn't know what they were or how they were used. There was no training course. I was given a manual and told, "This is what you'll be working on." To say it was all Greek to me would not do justice to my initial impression. But slowly I began to catch on and after my security clearance was granted, I was given the job of writing a program that would track the orbits of ballistic missiles. There was some complicated math involved and three months later I had a program that was working, churning out reams of data. The input I used came from Air Force radar sites on the Aleutian Islands, which were tracking missile launches being conducted by the Russians on the Kamchatka Peninsula. "You're working on the defense of our country," my boss George told me. And I was proud!

In the first week of October, there was a sudden buzz of activity at our plant. I noticed a lot of Air Force officers prowling about the premises as I was summoned to my boss's office. "Take these coordinates and plug them into your program," he said. So I trudged off to the computer room, sat at an IBM keypunch, and entered the data on input cards for my program. I was soon back at my boss' office with the output data. "These are strange," I said. "There's no impact point." "Right," he said as he closed the door behind me.

I finally came to the realization that my program was one of the first in the nation to calculate the orbit of Sputnik, which had gone up the day before. It didn't seem like a big deal then, but, looking back, I like to think it was.

My boss George was a born again Christian who carried a tiny bible in his shirt pocket. He never tried to proselytize me but the few times the subject of religion came up he would pull out his little book and read me chapter and verse. He quickly demonstrated he knew a lot more about the bible than I did. Catholics were always discouraged from studying the bible lest we go astray by misinterpreting what we read.

One thing I really liked about my job was the availability of overtime. The Cold War was in full flower and money was no object. One rush-rush, hush-hush project I worked on involved producing a set of tables that would be used in case of a computer failure at a remote radar installation in the Aleutians. The idea was that a technician could use tables to manually calculate the impact point of a ballistic missile if the computers were down. I was told on a Friday evening that the tables had to be ready by Monday morning. I worked all Friday evening, most of Saturday and Sunday to finish the job. Computer time was very expensive back then, costing some $2,000 an hour on the mainframe. I used some $50,000 of computer time on that weekend alone! When the engineers tested the tables, they found the fastest anyone could manually calculate impact points was forty-five minutes, that is if he didn't make any mistakes along the way. The upshot was that a missile fired at the US from Russia would impact some thirty to forty minutes later. In other words, by the time the warning would have been sounded, the explosion would have already taken place! I jokingly said, "If the technician wants to know the impact point, tell him to stay tuned to the radio. He'll find out five minutes earlier." One of the engineers on the project announced to everyone at a staff meeting, "If you have a budget under-run on your project, call in Ellis." The Cold War follies produced a lot of waste.

In my first year working at GE, as you might imagine by now, I made an additional fifty-percent in wages on overtime. I was now ready to buy a house and my wife and I began looking at real estate advertisements. We found a nice two-story, three bedroom house that was closer to my job, and for the grand sum of $12,000 we became part owners of the American dream.

I was somewhat ambitious I admit and was always looking for ways to climb the ladder at GE. I anticipated that I would be spending my whole career with this company, a common practice back then. So, I worked hard and took on jobs that others were hesitant to do. A supervisory job opened up at the Farrell Road plant that no one else seemed to covet so I asked to be considered. "You don't want that job," my boss said. "It's a mess and a has whole bunch of complainers working there." But I dearly wanted a supervisory job and soon I was commuting to that plant some fifteen miles away.

It truly was a mess and the big boss was exasperated by the frequency of the complaints. I would be supervising a staff of only five people in a section that had two IBM 1401 computers and a tab room. The complaints from the plant's customers consisted mainly of job deadlines being missed. It didn't take long before I reorganized the operation and the complaints dropped to zero.

While out shopping one Saturday, I ran into my boss's boss and he took time to compliment me. "I don't know what you're doing out there," he said, "but I'm not getting any more complaints. Keep up the good work." I felt like someone on his way up the ladder.

My euphoria was short-lived. A new immediate boss was installed—a bean-counter who knew absolutely nothing about computers. GE was notorious for believing that a manager was a manager no matter what the business was. My new boss soon started getting complaints about me overstepping my bounds at the satellite plant—it seems I was giving people out there services that they should have been getting at the main plant. My clients were not bashful about bragging how they could get jobs done and programs written by me that they couldn't get done at the central facility. The manager at the main facility complained to my boss that I was subverting the system, which would consequently have a deleterious effect on the organization. And, that wasn't good according to my new boss. I was flabbergasted to say the least. So were my clients. Sounds kind of silly, I know, but that was my first introduction to the notion of turf wars.

When I was told that I had to cease and desist, I told my new boss that I would be quitting. The alarm was sounded up the chain after IBM called to ask permission to interview me. The people at the local office had seen what I was doing with their computers, utilizing them in ways that could only lead to more sales for them, so they wanted to hire me. GE was their largest commercial customer so they also wanted to make sure the company wouldn't be angry if I went to work for them. Soon thereafter my boss found a job for me with a GE consulting group in Schenectady, which I ultimately accepted. I then began an even longer commute that lasted some six months before we sold our house and relocated to Ballston Lake, New York.

The consulting group I joined was primarily peopled with men who had reached dead end jobs within some department of the far-flung GE empire. They were either too old to be considered for promotion or had had been passed over for one reason or another. Teams of up to four were continually on the road consulting with other GE departments or with any of the many large customers of the company. The job required nearly constant travel, so I had the opportunity to get to know my fellow team members quite well.

I thought it was both an interesting group and interesting work. It was where I, as the youngest team member, picked up some social skills that had long been neglected in my life. It was where I learned to drink martinis, eat hearty dinners, gain weight, and play bridge. It was also where I refined the art of drawing charts, giving presentations, and writing reports that companies put on shelves, never to be read a second time.

Frequent business travelers have many stories to tell—about close calls, unscheduled stops, cancelled flights, and bad weather. Some are humorous and others not so much. Once I was traveling with an older member of the team whose initials were RHH. He was called Hubie by everyone, a diminutive form of his given name Hubenthal. We were scheduled to go out on a Monday morning to Ely, Nevada to work on a job for the Kennecott Copper Company. The plane left Albany on time for NYC where we would board a TWA flight to Dallas and then a United flight to Salt Lake City, in time to take the only flight to Ely at 3:30 in the afternoon.

How it happened I have no idea, but the short flight to NYC lost a half hour in the air and we missed our connection to Dallas. I had already been frantically scouring flight schedules in the fat guide book that all airlines kept aboard. It was a skill I had gotten really good at because working around problems is normal procedure for computer programmers. I picked out a flight we could take to Chicago but we'd have to change terminals from TWA to United at O'Hare airport to catch the flight to Dallas. Having only twenty minutes to grab our luggage and hike over to the other side of O'Hare is a neat trick if you've never tried it. Perhaps only frequent flyers would appreciate the difficulty of this task.

Ever the thinker, I quickly hatched a plan. "Hubie," said I. "You take the tickets, get them exchanged, and meet me over at the United gate for the Dallas flight." "What are you going to do?" he asked. "Give me your claim ticket, and I'll get the bags and meet you over there."

Remember, this was before all the security and regulations we have in place now—the glory days of flying. After getting off the plane, I turned and went down the set of stairs that led out on the tarmac where our plane was being unloaded. I spotted my bag and told the handler I needed it as I was making a tight connection. I showed him my claim ticket and he handed it over. I then said there was one more bag and kept looking for a suitcase with Hubie's tag on it. Lo and behold, I spotted the bag with his initials RHH but the handles and tag were gone! They had been somehow ripped off back in NYC. Luckily I recognized it and convinced the handler that it was indeed the bag I was looking for. I put the somewhat dilapidated, handle-less bag under my arm, grabbed mine, and looked over the tarmac to see the target United terminal off in the distance. I said to one of the TWA employees that it would be worth a few bucks to me if I could be driven over to United.

There was a station wagon nearby so he grabbed the bags, threw them in the back, and said, "Jump in." He thereupon drove straight across the tarmac to United, deposited me next to the staircase leading up to the boarding gate, and wouldn't take any money. I arrived to a look of surprise from the startled gate attendant—he wasn't used to anyone approaching boarding from that direction. I mentioned that there would be two of us taking this flight and would he page my friend, which he did. Pretty soon, old Hubie was hustling towards our gate, out of breath and wondering just what the hell was going on. "I was standing in line to exchange our tickets," Hubie said, "when I heard my name called and to proceed to this gate. How the hell did you get over here so fast?" "It's a long story," I said. The United people took our TWA tickets and let us on board. Hubie looked down with sorrow at his treasured suitcase. "They're going to have to pay for this," he said.

Our odyssey was just beginning because the United flight had a scheduled stop in Memphis, thereby putting us in Dallas five minutes after the flight to Salt Lake was scheduled to take off. If we missed that, then we wouldn't make the last flight to Ely. Hubie came up with an idea: "I'll get off at the plane in Memphis and call United to tell them to hold the Dallas plane for us." I didn't know if they would do that, but stranger things than that happened back in those days.

After Hubie returned, I asked how the phone call went. "I got hold of them. They said they'd take care of us." I grabbed the scheduling bible again and began mapping alternative routes to see if we could get to Ely any other way. There was no other way. The window of opportunity had slammed shut.

Just as we touched down at Dallas, I looked out the port window and saw a United flight taking off. "There goes our flight, Hubie," I said. Sure enough, it had gone without us. When we got to the United counter the clerk said, "Are you the guys that called about holding the flight to Salt Lake? Well, we couldn't do that but we are going to take care of you." They let us use their plush flight club where we could relax while we waited for the next plane going to Salt Lake. It would put us in at 5:45 PM, well after the Ely flight had landed at its destination. "Don't worry," the attendant said. "We've made arrangements for ground transportation."

When we finally landed in Salt Lake, there was a man waiting for us who gathered up our luggage and took us to our ground transportation. "You'll be traveling on the Lewis Brothers Stage," he said. Visions of a western movie popped into my head and I couldn't help wonder just what this "stage" was going to look like.

We arrived at the Lewis Brothers Stage depot, went in, and bought our tickets. Turned out the stage was an International Harvester station wagon, loaded with small packages that would be delivered to businesses along our route. When the driver got in, he looked back and said, "Oh, I've got passengers tonight." This was not a good omen.

Promptly at 6:00 PM, the stage took off and went to the Greyhound bus station, then over to the Trailways station, then over to the Salt Lake Hotel. The driver went into each place soliciting more passengers. He found none. Right at 6:30, we arrived back at the Lewis Brothers Stage depot. We'd been on the road for a half-hour only to return to where our journey began. This too was not a good omen.

The driver returned because there were two old ladies who had spent the day shopping in Salt Lake and now were headed back home to Arthur, a little town about twelve miles away. Once on the road, our stage stopped at every corner gas station and drug store within thirty miles of Salt Lake. The driver would drop off an auto part here, a case of Coke syrup there, continuing this routine until we hit the open road. Our first major stop was at a diner in Wendover, Nevada, just across the Utah border. This would be where our driver would trade vehicles with the guy coming from Ely, who would then drive us on to our ultimate destination.

The Bonneville Salt Flats aren't that scenic during the day, much less so at night. We arrived at our hotel in Ely at 1:00 AM, and factoring in the time change, we had now been on the road for over twenty hours. I could only imagine what it was like in the olden days when people made this journey on real stages—with horses!

Had there been frequent flyer mileage rewards in those days, I would have racked up thousands. I'm also sure

GE would have made me turn them in to the company for use on future business trips.

It was considered normal practice for the consultants to fly out on Sunday night and return the following Friday evening. If we traveled west of the Mississippi, we had to stay out for two weeks. Plane tickets were too expensive, or so the company said. I once spent the Easter holiday in Arizona because of the two-week rule. Another interesting experience I had was when coming back from Cincinnati, trying to make the last flight out of Idlewild (about six months before it was renamed John F. Kennedy Airport) to Albany. If I didn't make my flight, which happened often in those days, I'd be stuck overnight in New York. When I got off the plane and was rushing down the gangway to change terminals, I heard someone calling out, "Passenger Ellis, Passenger Ellis!" I said, "I'm passenger Ellis." There were two uniformed attendants, one of whom grabbed my bag and said, "Is this all your luggage?" "Yes," I responded. They hustled me out a door, put me into a station wagon and started driving around the airport loop. I noticed that they went past my terminal so I hollered, "You've gone by it!" The attendants looked at each other and then the driver said, "Aren't you passenger Ellis who is going out on Air India?" "No," I said. "I'm passenger Ellis who is going to Albany." They both began to laugh uproariously, then turned onto an off ramp and took me back to my terminal. As I exited they said, "Have a ride compliments of British Airways." I couldn't help but laugh myself, wondering how stupid they must have thought I was. Who would have believed that a small trunk airline was ferrying its passengers between

A Good Day for Flying

terminals? Just me, I guess.

What I found most interesting about our consulting group was the many quirks I saw in the people I worked with. George, who became the second born again Christian boss I'd had with the same name, was positively anal about appearances and orderliness. He was partial to bow ties, just like the prior George, and was often joked about by the more worldly members of the crew. "He wouldn't say shit if he had a mouthful of it," said Smitty, one of the oldest guys in the group. George also strongly believed in confidentiality, closing his office door for all phone calls, interviews, and meetings. This irked Smitty who one day decided to pull a prank on George by taping a Playboy centerfold to the back of his office door. When he closed it for his next meeting, the bunny would practically smack him in the face.

When his next interview took place, we listened to hear a reaction as George closed his door, but there was none. I asked the new hire how George had reacted. "He didn't say anything. I could see he was taken aback, but he let it hang there and went on with the interview, just as if nothing had happened." It wasn't what Smitty expected, but we got a chuckle out of it anyway. George, independent of his beliefs, was hard to rattle.

I traveled with George on a few occasions and got to observe him fairly close up. A more honest guy I have never met, although his goody-two-shoes demeanor wasn't a lot of fun on the road. He actually enjoyed a beer now and then, and let me in on the secret he used to keep beer cold in his motel room. He'd buy a six-pack at a grocery store and store the beer in his bathroom's toilet tank. "Keeps them nice and cool," he said. Although I was fairly frugal myself, I never went that far.

George came out to Ely once to observe the Kennecott Copper team in action. After our work day was over, everyone would traipse over to the Green Lantern for a beer. George came along because he knew fraternizing with customers was good for business. What the poor guy didn't know was that this establishment was a perfectly legal Nevada brothel. George's straight-laced attitude was known even to the Kennecott employees, and one guy who was a regular at the Green Lantern and knew all its personnel, conjured up a prank to play on him. He got one of the working girls to corner George, planting her hands on the wall, and rubbing up against him purring, "What do ya say big boy, wanna' fuck?" We all got a laugh as George turned beet red and began stammering incomprehensibly. "Golly" was a favorite expression of his and he was heard to utter this several times that night.

I modeled the following story after my old boss George even though it is set in Florida.

A Good Day for Flying

"A GOOD DAY FOR FLYING," George thought as he exited his car. A high-pressure area accompanied by a gentle, western breeze yielded a rare cloudless sky for Central Florida. He parked in the airport's short-term lot even though he'd be gone three days and three nights. It would cost twice as much but his company would pay because of the inconvenience he suffered for traveling so often and on such short notice. To the thirty-six-year-old manager in a growing high-tech company, this was a simple optimization of the cost and convenience variables. The Nebraska farm-boy, cum engineer, knew about these things. That was the way his mind worked.

As he strode to the terminal, garment bag slung over his shoulder and briefcase in hand, the slender, 5'11" engineer had to remind himself where he was. In a life of frequent flying, all airports had begun to look the same to him. "No turbulence today," he thought as he looked up at the sky, a bit apprehensively. The picture of the previously studied weather map flashed across his mind's computer screen. His brain was a prodigious signal-processing device that always stored the weather forecast on flying days in his large memory bank. "No turbulence today," he repeated. George knew about these things.

The escalator up to the main lobby was crowded with tourists of all dimensions going in all directions. Men and women who had obviously never seen themselves in rearview were dressed in shorts and flip-flops, trailing strings of kids with Mickey Mouse ears atop sunburnt faces. They surged five abreast through the airport corridors, carrying and dragging luggage, laden with shopping bags and stuffed animals, making it impossible for the impatient George to easily get by. He had often timed how long it would take from his house to the airport gate in order to minimize wait times before takeoff. But these attempts at efficiency often went for naught because of the ever-increasing human traffic at Orlando International Airport. So George reconciled himself to the discomfiting din and jockeying required to reach the tram that would take him to his appointed gate. This was the price he had to pay for working in paradise, one of the most popular tourist destinations on earth.

The impatient traveler wiggled his way into line for the security check behind a large woman who insisted on trying to pass through the metal detector with her purse. "Will they never learn?" George thought. Others forgot to take off their shoes—a requirement that George found particularly stupid. He didn't like having to take his laptop out of its case either, but these were the nuisances that airport security had inflicted on hapless travelers. What people tried to carry on a flight also continually amazed the engineer. Weight was just another of the flying variables that concerned him. He took to silently observing and criticizing the obesity of his fellow passengers and the amount of baggage they carried even though he knew it was a futile exercise. He was convinced that a crash of a commuter plane in the past year was attributable to overloading, and his on-board computer replayed the weight limits that his scheduled plane could safely carry. Yes, George knew about these things.

As usual, his assigned boarding area was overcrowded, so the ever-efficient engineer shunned his designated gate in favor of an adjoining one that was unused at the moment. There he could stretch his legs without fear of romping kids tripping over him or his briefcase. Also, as usual, he would be the last to board, always waiting for final call and the gangway to be clear of the over-anxious, inexperienced travelers. Finally, he inched down the aisle of the Boston-bound plane, past the people who had finally crammed their belongings into the overheads, to claim his seat in the mid-section of the plane. The baggage compartments were always jammed full so he knew better than to try finding room there for his garment bag and briefcase. They would have to fit under the seat in front of him, the only area he could call his own.

Once the plane had taxied into position for takeoff, George instinctively changed his digital chronograph to timer mode. He awaited the surge of the engines straining for full power and the release of the brakes, events that signaled him to press the watch's start button. As the plane sped faster and faster down the runway, he watched the seconds tick off on his Seiko.

Twenty-four . . . twenty-five . . . twenty-six . . . "Up, up," he whispered. George knew that if this aircraft wasn't airborne in thirty-five seconds, it was all over, off the end of the runway and a horrible crash. Every time he flew he timed the takeoffs and he knew the margin of safety, the envelope in engineer's parlance, for all the various commercial jets. This one was up in thirty-five or he stood a good chance of not being alive. Thirty . . . . Was it up? Yes, yes, it was and the steep angle of attack prompted a quick glance out the window to confirm that the craft was indeed airborne. He had survived another takeoff. George blew an involuntary sigh of relief. Good engineers did things by the numbers and this ex-farm boy of solid German stock was indeed a good engineer.

The furtively apprehensive traveler now glanced about the cabin. How many people here know how close to death they are on takeoff, he wondered. He reckoned that most of his fellow passengers were indifferent to the workings of the machines that were the backbone of the infrastructure of civilized society. His inquisitive mind, however, had to know how things worked. But unfortunately, his knowledge often became his psychological enemy because he also knew how easily things could, and often did, go wrong. He tried to be fatalistic about it at first, to no avail. His logical brain was effortlessly overpowered by his emotional instinct for survival. In truth, although loath to admit it, the man was afraid to fly.

As if it took one to know one, George could easily recognize other white-knuckle flyers. They death-gripped the armrests and stared straight ahead, as if sheer willpower could lift the plane off the ground or steer it out of danger. But the proud engineer could barely admit his phobia to himself much less to anyone else. It just wouldn't do. He was a man controlled by intellect, not emotion, so he went to great lengths to mask his true feelings, covertly patting the damp spots on his forehead with his handkerchief, as he inventoried the material in the seat pocket in front of him.

"Hmm . . . no barf bag," he noticed. Well that would be okay because he hadn't actually been airsick in quite some time. The airline magazine wasn't of interest to him because he had already seen it at least twice before. They only changed once a month and he flew far too often to expect to see new issues on every trip. Besides, the articles were too shallow for a man of his intellectual curiosity. A cursory look at the pamphlet describing this particular aircraft's configuration verified the most important facts he already knew—the location of flotation devices and the emergency exits. So, he reclined his seat and closed his eyes. Knowing that he couldn't sleep on an airplane at five in the afternoon wouldn't prevent him from trying. But, after a half-hour he conceded that his anxiety had won again, sat up and decided he might as well do some paper work. Just as he was about to reach under the seat in front of him to pull out his briefcase, a soft voice interrupted him.

"Do you fly a lot?" The question came from the

window seat next to his.

George had briefly glanced at his pretty seatmate when boarding, but had since avoided looking at her. He now took a closer look and decided that a) she was quite young, maybe eighteen, b) that she was an inexperienced flyer, and c) that she was extremely good looking. Now, on further scrutiny, he decided the fair-skinned blond could be as old as twenty-five. "Yes I do," he answered. "As much as I care to."

"Isn't it wonderful? This is only my second flight."

George thought that rather unusual in this day and age. If she was eighteen it was plausible, but not if she was twenty-five. "Have you been vacationing?" he asked. "Do Disney and all that business?"

"Oh, yes. I've been on break from grad school. My first flight was on the way down. It was marvelous."

George reflected on his first flight. He never quite thought of it as "marvelous." In fact, although he wouldn't tell anyone, he was sick as a dog and scared to death. "What are you studying?" he asked, wanting to change the subject to something other than flying. He decided that engaging her in conversation might be a pleasant diversion from the papers in his briefcase. The Valium he'd popped before boarding had finally relaxed him to a point where he felt comfortable in conversing with a complete stranger.

"I'm a psychology major, at Harvard, going for my PhD."

"Really, what branch of psychology? Experimental, applied, clinical?" George knew about these things.

"You aren't by chance a psychologist, are you?" she asked.

George couldn't decide if he should be flattered or offended. "Oh, no," he said. "I'm an engineer, electronics engineer." He had a fleeting worry that revealing his occupation might put a damper on the conversation, knowing that many younger people regarded engineers as nerds, gear-heads who wore white socks with brown shoes and carried plastic pen holders in their shirt pockets. He unconsciously shifted his feet forward to reveal that both his hose and shoes were black, in fashionable keeping with the blue suit he had on.

"Well, I don't know anything about engineering," she said. "I had all I could do to pass my math and science courses. I've always admired people with that aptitude."

"I was fortunate," George replied with a twinge of relief, even though he always felt anyone could master science if they put their mind to it. He reflexively pushed his glasses up the bridge of his nose in order to focus his vision more sharply on the image beside him. The young woman had almond-shaped, azure eyes and straight white teeth that were framed by a stunning smile. George hadn't concentrated this much attention on a woman in a long, long time. His eyes inconspicuously glanced at her left hand to see if a wedding band was among the many rings that she wore. "This is silly," he thought. "She's got to be ten to fifteen years younger than I am."

"When I was younger I wanted to be an airline attendant," his seatmate continued, "but my dad convinced me it would be a waste of my talents. I suppose he was right, but it would have been kind of exciting, traveling all the time, don't you think?"

Trying to be suave, George chose his answer carefully. "It's quite subjective, I guess," he answered. "To me, it would be a bit boring but I could understand how you might be attracted to it." In truth he couldn't offhand think of a worse occupation.

"Does your family mind you traveling all the time?" she asked.

"There's just me," George responded, not wanting to go into the painful details of being divorced four years ago by a wife who could stand neither his perfectionism nor his being away from home as much as his job required. He didn't know any woman well enough to talk about it. Not yet anyway.

"Oh," she said, putting away the textbook that had been in her lap since takeoff. "Well you must like traveling then."

George tried to change the subject again. "Well enough," was all he could say. "By the way, I went to school in Boston, MIT," he added.

"Did you?" she gushed. "Isn't that a coincidence?"

The conversation for the next twenty minutes included rapid exchanges about the ambiance of MIT versus Harvard, dinner at Lochober's, concerts on the Esplanade, and the exploits of the Red Sox and Celtics. For the first time in a very long time George was enjoying conversation with a woman, and a total stranger at that. He was impressed with the diversity of her interests and, aside from her infatuation with air travel, thought her mature and sophisticated beyond her years.

Suddenly, the plane hiccoughed violently as if it had gone over a bump in the sky. George took sharp notice, quickly leaning forward to glance out the window. An alarm sensor in his brain started going beep, beep, beep, and "Losing altitude!" blinked across his mind's computer screen. The signals were quickly sent to the palms of his hands, and they responded by emitting clammy beads of sweat. His head swiveled and his eyes darted to the back of the cabin to see if there was any unusual activity among the flight attendants.

"Wow . . ." his seatmate exclaimed. "That was fun."

George didn't respond, but noticed a perplexed attendant talking on the intercom to the flight deck. Beverage service, which was at mid-plane, was quickly buttoned up, carts wheeled forward and hurriedly stowed in their proper place. "The captain has advised that we must curtail beverage service at this time," the loudspeaker intoned. "There is the possibility of turbulence so please observe the seat belt sign and place seat backs and trays in their upright positions."

George thought, "This could be serious." His hands involuntarily gripped the armrests more securely. The plane had definitely lost altitude and had done a slow 180-degree turn. The psychology major studied George's change in demeanor and when he noticed her frowning at him, mustered a weak smile.

"Is anything wrong?" she asked in a voice now embroidered with concern.

"No, no," George replied as calmly as he could. "Everything's okay."

The loudspeaker came alive again. "This is your captain speaking. There is no reason to be alarmed but we've encountered a problem. One of the engines has overheated, and I've had to shut it down. This Boeing 737 can fly on one engine so there's nothing to worry about. I've decided to land at the nearest airport, just as a precaution. So just sit back and enjoy the trip. We're going to put down at Greenville, North Carolina, that's closest to us. So relax folks, everything's going to be fine."

George listened to every inflection in the captain's

voice. He was sure he heard the copilot say mayday in the background while the captain was speaking. "He said mayday!" his ear shouted to his brain. "He said mayday! They're lying! We're going down!"

Just as panic was about to take complete control of him he felt the woman's hand on his arm. "Are we in trouble?" she asked, as all traces of the pleasure and excitement of flying simultaneously drained from her face and voice.

George could see that her vivacity and ebullience had quickly been overpowered by fright. After a reflexive wipe of his right palm on his pant leg, he took her hand in his and spoke soothingly to her, surprising himself in the process. "Now don't you worry, we'll be all right. This will go down in memory as a minor inconvenience." He wished fervently that this were true as he leaned forward again to look out the window past the trailing edge of the wing. He was sure there was a trail of smoke coming from the port engine. Someone in the rear of the plane shouted, "The engine's on fire!" This was followed by muffled screams up and down the aisle.

George's seatmate began to sob softly, so he took his right hand and gently stroked her long, honey-colored hair. "There, there," he said. "It's going to be all right. Trust me."

"I don't want to die," the girl sobbed as she rested her head on George's shoulder. "I'm too young to die. Tell me we're not going to die."

Although he also felt he too was too young to die, George reached for an inner reserve that he didn't know he had, trying to calm the young lady, whose name he didn't even know. "Listen," he said. "I know about these things, and everything's going to be all right."

"Are you sure?" she asked tearfully. "You're not just saying that, are you?"

"No, no," he lied. "You'll look back on this one day and laugh."

All the while, George kept an eye peeled out the window, instinctively wanting to brace himself for the inevitable impact. "Was that a runway?" he asked himself. "God, I think we're going to attempt a landing!"

Suddenly, they felt the thump of landing gear against concrete. The plane was rolling, rolling, rolling . . . as if it would never stop. The thrust-reverser of the remaining engine strained to stop the craft before reaching the end of the runway. The grinding of brakes screamed out for all to hear and slowly, slowly . . . the fishtailing plane came to a stop. Fire engines racing alongside quickly laid a spray of foam on the errant engine. The flight attendants popped open the emergency doors and the passengers were told to calmly but quickly slide down the inflated chutes.

"Leave all your belongings behind! And remove your shoes!" the voice commanded. Tourists who automatically reached up to the overhead bins had to be chided to leave their prized vacation souvenirs where they were. George hurriedly led the young woman to the nearest forward exit and gently urged her down the slide ahead of him. When they hit the ground, he took her by the hand as they ran away from the plane.

"Oh my God, oh my God," she said when they had gone a safe distance. "We made it!" Impulsively the woman, who was nearly as tall as George, threw her arms around him and gave him a big hug. George, limp with relief, hugged her back.

In the airport lounge where the buses had brought

them, George and the young woman stood in their stocking feet looking out the big picture window. They alternately glanced at the setting sun and at each other. "I don't even know your name," he said.

"It's Melanie," she laughed. "I'm so glad you were with me. I don't know what I'd have done without you. You were such a tower of strength."

"My name's George by the way," he said as he gazed at Melanie, not being able to break his trance. Reluctantly, he then added, "You probably won't believe this but . . . I was more scared than you were." Melanie looked back at him incredulously as he added, "Yes, yes, it's true. I've always been afraid to fly," he confessed as the words caught in his throat.

Melanie let George rest his head on her shoulder and gave him another hug as the dying sun's rays poured into the terminal, making a large silhouette of their embrace for all to see. This was a moment he knew he would cherish forever.

Oh yes, George knew about these things.

The path not taken

8

MY CAREER WITH GE CAME TO A close shortly after I got an unexpected call one Sunday afternoon from a friend down in Arizona. This former co-worker had designed a toy computer and when discussing the marketing of his invention with a Wall Street type, he was asked what he did on his day job. Computer was a mesmerizing word back then and the Wall Street guy said he knew some people who might want to finance a startup in the fledgling timesharing business—sharing computers, not real estate. Back then, computers were quite expensive and software had been developed that allowed more than one user to access the same machine at the same time.

My friend said that he had been offered financing for a startup and would only do it if I came along. When I told my boss what I was thinking, he said I was making a big mistake. He got his boss, the VP of finance, to invite me to GE headquarters at 570 Lexington Ave in New York for lunch and a chat. "We've got big things planned for you," he said. "Why, next year you'll go to Crotonville." Everyone knew that was where the company cultivated its general manager corps. It certainly gave me pause and caused me to agonize over my decision for several days.

Six weeks prior, my boss had unexpectedly invited me join him in the conference room at the office. To my surprise, GE President and Chairman Gerald L Phillipe was seated there. "Flip," as his company intimates knew him, rose with a smile to greet me and said he'd heard a lot about me. Of course, I was flattered because this was the first time I'd ever met anyone that high up in the corporate echelon. Flip was an Iowa farm boy who'd made that improbable climb up the company ladder, carving out a name for himself among the barons of the business world. I found the man surprisingly affable and congenial—his success wasn't worn on his sleeve, and he quickly put me at ease.

Flip bade me to be seated and we chatted for a while, but I can't remember about what. When the meeting was over, I walked out of the conference room on a cloud. I was on my way! Why, the company president knew my name! All those long hours and hard work were finally going to pay off. I couldn't wait to get home to tell my wife.

Alas, my euphoria was short-lived. Just two weeks later, Phillipe was giving the commencement address at some university and suddenly fainted—striking his head on the podium as he fell. He suffered a subdural hematoma they said, and the next morning he was dead. This was a great shock to GE employees, especially me. The man who knew my name was no more. What was equally shocking was that the stock market greeted the news with a long yawn. It didn't even have the respect to drop the price of GE shares a quarter point for old Flip. I couldn't help but wonder, "What I could be worth?"

I had just celebrated my tenth anniversary with the company, and there was a lot on my mind that June morning as I was driving to work. I always took the back roads to the plant to avoid traffic tie-ups, which were becoming more and more common on the main drag. The less-traveled route that I used took me by an imposing old folks' home, set far up on a hill beyond a yawning expanse of lawn. Suddenly, the glancing rays of the rising sun drew my eyes towards an array of lawn benches up near the home's entrance. I don't know what compelled me, but I quickly pulled over to the shoulder of the road and stopped.

I had passed this place hundreds of times over the previous five years and hadn't given it much notice. And I certainly never stopped before. But now, as I looked at the scene that stretched out before me, I saw what had caught my eye. A silver-haired, elderly gent was sitting on one of the benches, his head tilted back, face soaking up the warming waves of the morning light.

"What can he be thinking?" I wondered. "Is he reflecting on his past life?" I wondered at my inquisitiveness. "Is he pondering the road not taken? What will I be thinking if and when I reach that point in life? Will I have regrets or satisfaction?"

I quickly divined the reason for my unusual and impulsive act. It was because the life-changing decision I had been sub-consciously pondering for two weeks running was lodged in my brain, suffusing my thoughts.

I put my car into drive and continued on to work. That would be the very day I handed in my resignation. I couldn't imagine being in that old man's shoes one day, looking back into the dim past, wondering what would have happened if I had not taken this step. Win or lose, this was what I had to do, and I thanked that gray-haired old gent for making me pause to ponder the notion of the path not taken.

The bottom line is that I chucked my rising career at GE. I must admit that it wasn't only a drive to satisfy my entrepreneurial instincts, but also a concern about General Electric that had been nagging me for some time. The company had been taken over, and was run by, accountants. If there's anything those bean counters believe in, it's the gospel of fiduciary responsibility.

About midway into my GE career, I developed a theory about the evolutionary stages a company goes through before it finally dies. Looking at American corporate history I saw that most companies started out with the inventor, or developer of the idea, as the head of the new enterprise. In fact, Thomas Edison, one of the most prolific inventors in American history, was the founder of General Electric. This first stage in a company's evolution is what I called the engineering phase. As the enterprise grows and sales increase, the company realizes the need to find ways to produce its products faster and less expensively, so it enters the manufacturing stage. Once it knows how to make the widgets faster and cheaper, it begins to focus on how to sell more and more of its goods, and enters the marketing phase. Once sales begin to slow down, the company begins to focus on how to improve profitability, and enters the accounting phase. That's the stage GE was in when I went to work for them.

If you think about it, when a company reaches that level of maturation, it is not the best environment for nurturing new ideas, or the development of new products. The accountants know numbers and can plot trends for sales and expenses till the cows come home. They don't know how to produce or sell more, but how much it costs to do so. In the final analysis they create nothing other than paper. As in the biblical aphorism, "Consider the lilies, how they grow: they neither toil nor spin." In my view, when a company reaches the lily stage, they are on their way to extinction. The final phase is reached when they put lawyers in charge to focus on the disposition of assets and all the legal wrangling that ensues on the road to death.

It didn't take long for me to see that if you worked at GE, and didn't pay attention to costs, then you weren't paying attention, period. The management knew the costs of everything—from cotter pins to aircraft engines. They went over expense reports with a fine tooth comb. Every expenditure had to be justified several times over. I used to half-jokingly say that we spent fifty cents justifying every dollar actually approved. I once suggested that if we just went ahead and spent the dollar, and it proved worthless then we'd be out just the dollar. However, by justifying it we could be out a dollar and a half. Unfortunately, the company didn't seem to know the value of quality, employee morale, or customer satisfaction. Perhaps the culture has changed in the years since I left.

I once got into a dispute with the consulting group's finance manager over a 15¢ expenditure for a newspaper that I had put on my expense account. This was an explicitly prohibited expense, and I wanted to test the system. My belief was that while I was on the road I had an obligation to keep up with current events. GE's thinking was that I should have my wife save the old newspapers, which I could read after I got home. "Not allowed," said the finance manager. "I want to appeal," said I. The big boss was annoyed. "Give the waitress an extra tip," he told me. I delighted in telling the finance guy, "He told me to lie!" Do you think more than 15¢ was spent on this dispute?

I also got into a jam with the marketing manager over a report that I had written. I was charged with examining a unit of the company's computer department in Phoenix, Arizona and found a whole host of problems, including a manager who didn't have a clue as to what his people were doing. I wrote a rather critical assessment and when he saw it, the marketing guy threw a fit. "How am I supposed to get consulting contracts with this kind of report?" he hollered. I stood my ground, even with the big boss who tried to adjudicate the squabble. He was sympathetic but in the end they softened the language considerably before giving it to the customer. The marketing manager cringed whenever I was sent out on a job.

Not many people remember that GE was in the computer business, a resource intensive enterprise that was still in its infancy. When its financial performance didn't improve quickly enough, they put one of their managers from the motor department in charge. "Costs," he said. "That's the problem!" His initial management thrust was concerned solely with controlling those costs. One of his first edicts was that everyone, in order to get a new pencil, had to turn in the old stub. One wag said, "So is this how we're going to beat IBM?"

GE was also an early pioneer in semiconductors. But the business was taking a long time to show a profit, while consuming large amounts of developmental funds. The company also entered the computer timesharing business when few people knew what that was. They got into the business largely because of software developed by one of its customers. They couldn't see its enormous potential and attacked it just like the many other businesses under its umbrella. They milked the fledgling idea dry and soon smaller companies came along and ate their lunch. GE silently exited the business.

Bottom line, to which GE people continually like to refer, the company got out of semiconductors, computers, and timesharing primarily because their bookkeepers lacked vision and were unwilling to invest in the future. Even if they had understood it, I doubt they would have invested what was required to nurture and develop those businesses. I think anyone who follows the stock market would agree that it would be difficult to find industries that experienced more explosive growth than these three did in the decades that followed.

So, I left my promising career at the big company for a fling in a risky undertaking that was financed with $350,000 in venture capital. This is considered a modest sum in those circles. Several other companies that were started with twenty times that amount, ultimately failed.

I was named the executive vice-president in charge of Marketing for the new Pittsburgh company named On-Line Systems. Everyone knows about being online today but back then it was a foreign word that hadn't yet entered the popular lexicon. Once when I was applying for credit at one of the city's department stores, the clerk after viewing my application asked, "Timesharing, is that a trucking company?"

The venture was soon deemed successful enough to take the company stock public and was traded on the NASDAQ, only a year after its founding. Turning nothing into something can be very stressful, and it took its toll on all of us. I was regularly working eighty-hour weeks and the long hours were beginning to show with tempers fraying on a regular basis. My tenure with the company began to unravel when I found that my partner, who was named president because he found the funding, was somewhat insecure about his role. In my marketing position, I often had to give presentations to financial analysts in various major cities. I used my previous consulting experience to prepare pretty charts for what we called "dog and pony shows." Our investment bankers had organized a presentation for a group of Wall Street types, and for which I had prepared a nice set of flip charts. I made the mistake of giving a preview to a few of the investment bankers before the planned lunch at Oscar's, across the street.

The bankers were enthralled with the look of the presentation, but it turned out my partner felt threatened. On the way across the street he told me that it would be best if he gave the presentation. Instead of objecting, I said, "Be my guest." That was a big mistake because he completely butchered my talk—he didn't know what he should be saying from chart to chart—and it went over badly. The lead investment banker said afterwards, "We've got to be better prepared next time."

It was foolish of me to allow that to happen so the next time something big came up that we disagreed on,

I didn't give in. There was talk of merger with a similar company that wasn't doing well and after performing due diligence, I thought it would be a mistake to combine with them. My partner, his insecurity showing, badly wanted to do the deal and asked me to support it at the next day's board meeting. I told him I wouldn't and offered to resign instead. The board accepted my resignation and, ironically, they never did the deal. The object of the company's affection went out of business shortly afterwards.

I wasn't sure what my next career move should be but was in no hurry to take another job. It was summertime so I decided the family would take a long vacation even though I had an offer pending for a position with the university of Pittsburgh, and told them I'd call in from somewhere along the way.

I bought a trailer, had a hitch put on our station wagon, and we embarked on a cross-country trip. My wife and our five young children logged 7,500 miles over a three week period, taking in the many sights to be seen across America. We stopped at places such as Mammoth Cave, The Painted Desert, Grand Canyon, Disneyland, Golden Gate Bridge, Fisherman's Wharf, Mt Shasta, Great Salt Lake, and other points of interest too numerous to mention.

While we were sitting around a campfire one evening, I decided to accept my next job with the University—where I would spend the next ten years directing their computer activities.

Entering academic life was fairly energizing for me because because I looked forward to an environment where logical arguments would be appreciated and intellectual discussions would be encouraged. It turned out I was to be somewhat disappointed. As one who took pride in my vocabulary, I was chagrinned when one PhD committee member commented, "There he goes again, using those fifty cent words." Stunted language skills, it seems, were not solely the province of the US Army.

I have to say that there were a few aspects of the university environment that I really enjoyed. One was the social life because academics know how to throw parties where eclectic groups gather to dine and converse. Also, liking sports as much as I do, complementary season tickets at Pitt Stadium and flying with the football team to away games were things I looked forward to. Pittsburgh won the National Championship one of the years I was there, and my wife and I had a great time in New Orleans at the Sugar Bowl.

University types cultivate large social networks among their confreres, not just in the States, but around the world, and they like to travel. I got to visit other university computer centers in Lebanon, Jordan, Kuwait, and Egypt. I was usually billed as an American computer expert and got to speak to many faculty and administrators. A number of the people I met overseas had done graduate work at Pittsburgh so they were naturally quite cordial.

On a visit to the American University of Cairo, Dr Farkhonda Hassn, a Pitt Alum who headed the science department, suddenly asked me if I'd like to be on TV. She didn't really give me a chance to turn it down, so at the appointed hour I was trundled off to the building that housed the television studio. The show I was to appear on was called *The International Club*, hosted by an Egyptian movie star by the name of Samir Sabry. His show was a Middle Eastern version of *The Ed Sullivan Show.* From what I observed, it consisted of a variety of acts, including comedians, dancers, and singers. Back then, Egypt was just emerging from its embrace with Russia, and many of its buildings and infrastructure had long been neglected. When the theater lights were turned up during an intermission, I could see that the place was in really sad shape. The seats were really ratty, and many were even broken and unusable. I wouldn't have been surprised to see a rat run across the stage.

Finally, during one of the breaks, the host pointed in my direction and motioned me to approach. I went up to the stage and we got a chance to chat a bit before the cameras came back on. He said, "You're Lebanese I understand." "Well," I responded, "my parents came to America from Lebanon." "Okay," he said and the theater lights dimmed as the host began my introduction. Sabry was quite the linguist—his English was perfect and he spoke both Egyptian and Lebanese dialects of Arabic.

"We have here an American computer expert, Dr Raff Ellis whose parents emigrated to America from Lebanon," he began. He then turned to me and asked, "Do you speak Arabic?" I told him that I spoke "taxicab Arabic," meaning that I could get around on my own. Throughout our conversation he would pause and translate our conversation into Egyptian Arabic to his audience. Turning back to me he said, "Let's pretend that I am a Taxi driver, and we'll test your taxicab Arabic." He then began speaking to me in the familiar Lebanese dialect. "Where do you want to go?" I gave him a destination in Beirut and asked, "How much?"

"Five pounds," he said. I responded with, "One." He then haggled down to, "Three." I responded, "One and a half." When he translated this to the audience, a roar of laughter went up. "You really are Lebanese," he said. They do have quite a reputation for bargaining.

Another funny exchange took place when my host asked, "Is it true that in America they use computers to make a match between men and women?" I responded that some had tried this but it wasn't very successful. "Why is that?" he asked. "Because," I said, "even the computer cannot fathom the woman." This got a really good laugh from the audience.

The next day when I was at the airport on my way home, people were pointing at me. The show was very popular and many people recognized me as I walked through the lobby. When going through customs, I was given a hearty salute and waved through without even a cursory inspection. I have missed that kind of notoriety.

Another of the more memorable experiences working in academic life in the 1970s came as the result of the then rampant student turmoil. Protests were ongoing, buildings were being occupied, and the Hare Krishna kids were outside chanting *ad infinitum*. Unknown to me was that the university was regularly receiving bomb threats against our computer installation. Luckily, the Unabomber Ted Kaczynski hadn't yet started his campaign. I only learned about these threats at one of my scheduled board meetings when the vice chancellor of finance was in attendance. "Oh yeah," he said rather casually, "We get threats against you all the time. Hell, if we evacuated every time we got a bomb threat, we'd never get anything done." I was shocked that I had never even been apprised of these threats. "I have a solution," I said, "let's move your office from the ivory tower, down next to the computer center." The suggestion was greeted with loud laughter but it didn't have a chance of happening. And I still didn't get any notices of the many bomb threats that continued to pour in.

University life is different from industry in many ways, but often it's quite the same. Irresistible forces meet immovable objects on a regular basis and turf wars are as common there as anywhere else. So, the time came when I realized that I had done all I could to advance the computing capabilities of the university. I led a drive to build an off campus computer center, and pioneered the use of microwave communications from the main campus to the new facility. I also had over a hundred personal workstations installed while expanding computational capabilities many times over. It was time for a change.

My next stop was back to industry with a fairly large computer company, a firm that had become an industry darling. This company, whose computers were a mainstay of university computing, had been written up in all the business magazines as a phenomenal success story, which it was. This would turn out to be the worst career move I ever made. I had never before worked in an environment where there was so much fat and waste, far exceeding what I experienced in defense contracting. The company had grown so fast and had promoted so many people beyond their levels of competence that it had to take a downturn—the only question was when. I had such a dearth of confidence in the firm that I made a good piece of change by selling the stock short.

My stint at the new company lasted only a year, due in part because the vice-president who hired me left just six months after my arrival. When my year was up, I followed my old boss to the Canadian company that had hired him. That in turn led, one year later, to a startup in Florida, bankrolled by the parent company, a conglomerate that was heavily into the oil and gas business.

The company I headed would design and develop desktop computer workstations that would join personal and computer communications in the same machine. It was an idea I had long harbored that connecting executives with their staff members through the computer with both voice and electronic messaging would make a great product. The result was quite a technological achievement but, as it turned out, was too far ahead of its time. Executives in corporations of that period weren't computer literate and weren't about to change. Many of the board members of the parent company couldn't or wouldn't use computers if their lives depended on it, and they said so. I remember at the conclusion of a product presentation I gave to the board of the parent company, one executive seriously asked, "Why would I want one of those?" In emerging markets, I soon learned, it doesn't pay to be too far ahead of the curve.

High technology doesn't mix well with oil and gas as the metrics used by natural resources firms don't apply to high tech at all. It reminded me somewhat of my experience at GE. The business was changing too fast for their style of management and after only five years the conglomerate decided to divest itself of my company. I suddenly found myself retired and at another crossroad.

I didn't really have to work for a living so I went back to college to obtain a degree I had always wanted, an MBA. Because my bachelor's degree was in science, I was forced to take thirty hours of undergraduate business courses as a prerequisite for graduate school. I also had to take an entrance exam—the Graduate Management Aptitude Test (GMAT). There was a minimum score of 450 required to be accepted into the masters program. As I noted before, I was always a good test taker so this requirement didn't faze me. I studied, took the test, and awaited the results, which ended up exceeding my expectations. While standing around awaiting class, one of my classmates was lamenting the GMAT and how he had scored only 420. It was the second time he had taken it and when he asked me how I did, I said, "You don't want to know." But he and some of the others began insisting that I tell, which in all honesty I didn't want to do. However at their insistence, I relented. "If you really want to know," I finally said, "620." They thought I was some kind of genius.

Going back to school at my age would prove to be a lot of work and a lot of fun at the same time. Associating with younger kids energized me but some of my profs weren't too happy to see me in their classes. The questions I asked were somewhat vexsome as my experience regularly clashed with their theory. I could tell stories of skullduggery, unethical behavior, and manipulation of stock prices that the profs didn't know about. The real-life goings on among the captains of industry can be very disappointing. Some teachers actually encouraged my participation and solicited my input while others looked the other way when I raised my hand. One of the better teachers told me that I was "an intimidating presence," but he enjoyed having me in class nonetheless.

I went at my course work in the same manner I had attacked my undergraduate studies some thirty years before. I obtained my degree eighteen months after I started, although I never got to put into practice my newfound knowledge of the business world.

That's when I decided that my long dormant writing ambitions should take wing. I began by writing short stories about my experiences and reminiscences, some of which you have already read.

Living in Florida has many advantages—and disadvantages. The weather for the most part is salubrious and quite predictable. Once people know you are living in this version of paradise, you get a lot of visitors—people you haven't seen in years come to call. Also, relatives begin to think it would be a wonderful idea if grandma came to stay with you, to live out her remaining years. "It would be so much better than a nursing home," they would say. The problem they didn't recognize or understand was that nursing homes have twenty-four hour a day staff availability—for a reason: They are needed. Many a family estrangement can be laid at the door of this particular conflict of interest.

Father Will

9

IT WASN'T LONG AFTER ARRIVING IN Florida that old
acquaintances began popping up. My friend Peewee's
sister also lived in the area, not far from where I was
located. I heard via the grapevine that Father Will (nee
Peewee) was coming for a visit, so I called his sister after
he arrived and suggested that we'd like to have him over
for dinner. There was a lot of hemming and hawing but
he was finally persuaded, as long as I picked him up and
returned him afterwards. I consented.

I don't recall exactly how many years it had been since
we last met but it was at least twenty. Peewee had put on a
lot of weight and his cheeks bulged with the consequences
of many rich meals, without the concomitant benefit
of exercise. Said cheeks also had a rosy hue that told a
story of high blood pressure and looming heart disease.
(A few years later he underwent a quadruple bypass
procedure.) His conversation was stilted, and he began
taking offense at my offhanded comments about certain
aspects of religion. He especially got lathered up when
I singled out the born again variety, with which I'd
had some experience, for some modest opprobrium. It
seems Father Will had adopted the born again stripe

of Catholicism, in a group that also spoke in tongues, which I offhandedly offered was a bunch of hooey. I was aghast that my old friend and fellow prankster had taken a sharp right turn around the religion bend. But in retrospect, I should have seen it coming.

I had visited Peewee when he was a seminarian and he was his old, but somewhat cleaned-up, prank-pulling self. He was given to playing jokes on his fellow students and had been reprimanded for it. His transformation was set in motion as a result of his intellectual endowment. Recognizing they had a budding theologian on their hands, his religious order sent him to Rome to study— an honor reserved for the brightest among them.

Peewee was a gifted linguist and, having already mastered German, he soon added Italian and French to his repertoire. When his three year stint in Rome was up, he flew back to the States, landing in New York. Heading home to Carthage via bus, he alighted in Albany where I had persuaded him to stop on his way. I picked him up at the bus station and brought him home with me. I couldn't help but notice that the previously robust young man was now a gaunt shadow of his former self. He had developed a bleeding ulcer and looked quite unwell. The suit he had on was loose fitting and worn thin. I quickly decided to give him a welcoming gift of a new suit of clothes. He accepted without protest.

The next day, I took my friend to my favorite haberdashery and introduced him to my Italian tailor. The two soon struck up an animated conversation in the tailor's native tongue while the latter measured and chalked Father Will's new set of clothes. Normally, it would have taken a week to have a suit altered but when told that the priest would be here only one more day, Father Will's new friend promised his new suit would be made ready for the the next day. The man was so happy to have someone to converse with in modern Italian, that were it in his power, I think he would have given the priest the suit for free.

The freshly clothed priest couldn't help but beam as he looked in the mirror after donning his new attire. It was a lovely, impeccably fitted black suit that my friend truly appreciated. I put Father Will on a bus for home and later introspected on how much he had changed in the last three years. The carefree prankster had been literally bled out of him and only the shell of his former self remained. Such a pity, I thought. Did all that rubbing up against the hierarchy and dogma of the Church really make him a better priest? I didn't think so.

When I had Peewee over for dinner all those years later, I began reminiscing about old times with stories that I had told my children. Father Will disavowed any knowledge of those pranks and genuinely seemed as if he had completely blocked those events from his memory. I felt sad for him that so many good times had been erased from his consciousness.

Father Will's mom had come to Florida to live with his sister and soon thereafter she became a nursing home resident. The priest was hesitant about visiting, and his sister continually scolded him about it. He finally came for a visit shortly before she died. My characterization of his visit, along with a dose of literary license, is chronicled in the following short story.

The Whistler

"YOU'D BETTER COME DOWN HERE SOON if you want to see her alive," his sister had said on the phone a week before. "I can get any priest to say the funeral mass, so don't wait until she's dead." She'd made him feel guilty, and he felt a bit angry that his sister could still push his buttons that way.

Father William McGrath, thus goaded, flew down to Orlando to see his mom, perhaps for the last time. "Take her, God," he prayed at her bedside, not loud enough for her to hear—he didn't want to take the chance she could understand. "She's only suffering now, Lord," he continued.

His mother was in the latter stages of Alzheimer's disease, and the affliction had progressed to the point where conversation had become impossible. As he studied her eye movements, he wasn't at all sure she even recognized him. He girded himself against an encroaching feeling of despair. If all those years of studying theology had taught him but one thing, it was that this was the easiest and most dangerous of sins to which a devout person could succumb.

"You're trying to test me, aren't you, Lord?" the priest thought to himself as he walked down the nursing home steps and ambled over to his airport rental car. The drive back to his sister's house was slow and deliberate. He was in no hurry to get there and actually seemed pleased that, as a stranger, it would be easy to lose his way, delaying the journey even more.

As he traveled the roads, he noticed how the scenery in Florida was so different from northern New York, where he was born and raised. Gazing out on the flat land, with its palm-tree-lined circular lakes, made him forget his mother and dwell on the diversity and beauty of nature. He came upon a sign announcing a rest area and impulsively decided to stop. He pulled up next to a park bench that overlooked the lake, yanked off his Roman collar, and got out.

His mood, already reflective, became more so because of the tranquil setting, and he unconsciously began to whistle. He had tootled incessantly as a kid, a habit that was hard to break even as he grew older. He had worked diligently as a youngster to perfect several bird calls that he used to fool his friends into thinking some exotic feathered creature was nesting nearby.

The priest dusted the sand off a bench with broad strokes of his hand, unbuttoned his shirt and sat down. "I could read my Office," he mused, but was not really in the mood. The years of priestly discipline would normally have forced him to get this daily chore over with but somehow today it did not. Instead, he sat there staring out over the lake, a gentle warm breeze splaying across his face. The glancing rays of the setting sun warmed him and simultaneously buoyed his spirits, so much so that he soon forgot where he was and why he was there. The middle-aged man closed his eyes and soon became a boy again.

William McGrath was known as Peewee by practically everyone in his hometown—except his parents and teachers. Many of his friends never knew his actual given name because his boyhood antics and diminutive size were inextricably linked to his pseudonym. "Did you hear what Peewee did?" many kids would say. The lad was always doing something to call attention to himself, and that usually meant trouble. Oftentimes his mother would hear the knock of a village policeman at her door inquiring as to the whereabouts of her errant son. He had, on occasion, been accused of discharging firearms inside the village limits and shooting pigeons up in the old grain silo. He and his friends went on many excursions together, including Halloween when certain hi-jinks went wrong and caused some property damage. Peewee was seen almost everywhere around the village, except perhaps in jail—which he avoided only through sheer luck. Whenever confronted by the long arm of the law, Peewee always had a quick response and seemed able to talk his way out of any scrape. Nabbing Peewee, it was said, was like trying to pick up banana slices off the kitchen floor.

Father Will, as everyone knew him after ordination, would wince whenever his memory involuntarily turned back the pages of time. What passed for fun and games as a child was no longer funny to him as an adult, even less so as a priest. But the more he tried to hold back some of the lurid details of his youth, the stronger they came to the fore. The priest seldom, if ever, thought about his early years as a potential reform school inmate. He had grown considerably from his Peewee days and whenever he ran into a boyhood friend who instinctively brought up one of those disagreeable memories, he would quickly change the subject. His fellow clergy didn't know much about his family or his youth because these were unpleasant topics that he didn't discuss. Among the many things he didn't like to remember was how his dad was dominated by his mother, or he by his older sisters. He never connected the dots . . . that his home environment might have been responsible for the outrageous behavior he used to attract the attention he desperately needed.

The priest's thoughts now turned to his old friend, with whom he had spoken just the day before. It had been years since they had conversed, much less seen each other. When he got word of his visit, his friend called Peewee's sister's house to invite him to dinner, but Father Will declined. "Too busy with my mother and all," he said. "Maybe next trip."

The priest had also cringed when his friend launched into tales about the torment that Peewee had caused the nuns at Augustinian Academy. In particular, he didn't want to remember poor old Sister Dorothy in the eighth grade.

Augustinian's eighth grade was on the second floor and looked out across Mechanic Street to the village fire department. Whenever there was a fire, a klaxon would boom a deafening noise directly into the classroom, and all instruction was interrupted until it stopped. The horn, like a giant goose, would honk out a numeric code that told the volunteer firefighters approximately where the fire was. Two blasts, a pause, and three more would be a "23" and one could look at the fire department's code card to see what streets that number covered. Every fireman carried such a card in his wallet.

Yet, no matter what digits were transmitted, Peewee would jump up, run to the window and exclaim, "That's my neighborhood! I'm going to have to go home!" An exasperated Sister Dorothy would shout over the din of the electric goose, "Get back to your seat, young man!" And the prankster, amid the muffled snickers of his peers, would reluctantly return to his desk, muttering all the way that he was losing his home, along with all his personal possessions.

Of course, Peewee's penchant for mischief continued unabated no matter the abundance of admonitions he collected along the way. He spent a lot of time dreaming up pranks that would draw his classmates' attention and result in cherished admiration.

One of the more devious shenanigans Peewee came up with resulted from his accidentally discovering that he could whistle with his mouth closed. One day for some unknown reason, when he had a paperclip stuck between his lips, perhaps to use as a toothpick, he found when he extracted it that it left a tiny, imperceptible hole between his lips. He exhaled through his lips, heard a faint whistle, and decided to exploit this heretofore hidden skill. After he had perfected it to his satisfaction, he turned his attention to its employment.

In class one day, while affecting an inordinately angelic countenance and pretending to read a book, he began his furtive whistling career. Sister Dorothy's ears, if you could have seen them under her nun's wimple, perked up and her radar quickly scanned the room. Unable to pinpoint the source, she stood up and, using dead-reckoning as her navigation device, began walking around the room trying to hone in on the cause of the intrusion. No matter where she walked, the melody continued until the exasperated nun would shout, "Stop that infernal whistling!"

Peewee would then turn around and indignantly chide his classmates. "Yeah, cut that out." Sister Dorothy would, of course, tell Peewee to be quiet, that she would handle it. But, she never discovered the culprit and the whistling went on intermittently for the entire school year, halting only when Peewee tired of its use. It was somewhat ironic that Father Will was now having thoughts that God was testing him after all the tests he had put the poor nuns through.

The crunch of tires on the stone drive jarred the priest from his reverie as he looked up to see a sheriff's patrol car pull up alongside his vehicle. He thought it odd that the deputy didn't get out of the car, but just sat there staring at him. It was a little past five in the afternoon and while he was lost in thought, a few children had filtered into the park to play on the monkey bars and slides located nearby. Father Will hadn't really noticed them until just then.

It became a bit unnerving that the deputy continued to sit in his cruiser, engine running while staring at the priest who suddenly felt the need to get back on the road. As he rose to leave, the deputy quickly turned off his car's engine, got out and stood between the priest and his automobile. Father Will didn't know why he had suddenly become intimidated by the actions of the tall, sun-glassed, cowboy-hatted police officer. Perhaps it was a reflex due to the numerous times so long ago that he had been confronted by cops in his hometown.

The lawman eyed the priest from top to bottom, double-checking the black clothing that had caught his eye when he first pulled in. Even sans the collar, the trooper had decided this man was a cleric of some sort. As Father Will drew near, the deputy spoke. "That your car?" Since there was only one other car, the priest thought this an odd question. "Yes it is," he responded. "Is there a problem?" "I see it's a rental car. Could you show me some identification . . . please?" His first instinct was to ask why, but he suppressed the impulse. His sister, mindful of her brother's penchant for speeding, warned him that cops in Florida weren't like those up north. "You don't want to question them," she said. "That only causes trouble."

Reluctantly the priest reached into his coat pocket, retrieved his wallet, pulled out his identification, and handed it to the sheriff. The deputy intermittently glanced at it while looking up at the priest. "Father, is it?" he said in an accusatory manner. "I don't understand," Father Will replied. "What's this about?"

"Do you like watching children play?" the officer asked sarcastically. A chill ran down the priest's spine. "What do you mean?" he sputtered. "I didn't even know there were children here." "Oh," the lawman scoffed. "How could you miss them?"

Father Will slowly realized that he had become suspect, because he had innocently decided to rest and reflect in a strange place. He reddened as he suppressed the anger that comes to those who have been unjustly profiled as villains. He now couldn't help but remember back to when he'd been confronted by police as a kid, and how glibly he concocted stories to demonstrate his innocence. At this moment, he was at a loss for words. Reluctantly he stammered, "I'm just visiting and wanted to rest on my way home." "Well you'd better be on your way," the deputy commanded, and Father Will immediately got into his car. He was so unnerved by the experience that he fumbled to put the key in the ignition. Finally the car started and he pulled out of the park with a start, throwing gravel in a stream behind him.

Raindrops began to fall as the car headed down the highway and soon, what was a sprinkle turned into a deluge that seriously obscured his visibility. Father Will didn't know why but even this outpouring couldn't wash away the negative feelings he now harbored. As he slowly inched along his way, thoughts of his dying mother returned.

There was no escape from guilt it seemed, past or present.

Sloan Wilson
author of "The Man in the Gray Flannel Suit"

10

ONE OF THE FIRST THINGS I DID WHEN I took up writing seriously was to join a group of people with similar aspirations. One such group was being moderated by a famous author, whose name no one remembers, but all of whom can recall his best-selling novel—*The Man in the Grey Flannel Suit*. His name was Sloan Wilson, a man whose life and writing had seen better times. In his late sixties, he lived in a rent-free house in Winter Park, Florida given him by a patron of the arts. He supplemented his income by writing magazine articles and hosting a writing group. Sloan had suffered bouts of alcoholism throughout his life and was temperamental, curmudgeonly, and often crudely critical. I liked him a lot, and if I learned one thing from him it was to look at my work from the perspective of, "Would anybody like to publish this?" Getting published was the Shangri-La of writing as far as Wilson was concerned, and his last really successful novel, *A Summer Place,* had been published thirty years prior. It wore on him. He also had what was later diagnosed to be early stage Alzheimer's disease to which, after a long, slow decline, he succumbed fifteen years later.

Although this isn't something an author would necessarily be proud of, one of Wilson's books, *Ice Brothers*, was used by Unabomber Ted Kaczynski to conceal one of his explosive devices. The bomb was sent to the president of United Airlines and exploded when he opened the book, severely injuring him. It was never revealed why Kaczynski, considered by many to be a contemplative genius, chose that particular work.

The way Sloan ran his group was to read aloud work that anyone dared submit in advance. He would render his critical comments, and then, after setting the tone for the critique, would let other members of the group chime in with their thoughts. Many writers were hesitant to undergo this public raking over the coals and wouldn't submit their work for public scrutiny. Color me naive or stupid, but I gave him a narrative every week that we met. I enjoyed having the master read my stories, and took his criticisms to heart.

One of the stories I wrote that generated a lot of comment was about the angst of facing aging parents. For many, this experience can be very traumatic as the memories of past vibrancy are rudely replaced with the reality of present demise. This story was sketched out on notebook paper while I was riding the bus after a visit to my hometown. Although the story is dramatized, it is factually faithful to what I experienced.

After Wilson read it, one of the group's members, a screenwriter of some accomplishment, said it was reminiscent of a Eudora Welty story, and he meant it in a complimentary way.

Going Home

IT IS A LONG TRIP BACK HOME. A seemingly endless bus ride, but it's the only way to get there, unless I want to drive 1,500 miles. So I take a plane to get within ninety miles of the place and then catch a bus. It's all the longer because the creaky old bus seems to understand my reluctance and stops at nearly every intersection that's marked on the map.

Nearly everyone likes to go back home, at least for a visit. I guess I'm different. Even though it's where I was born and brought up with reasonably pleasant childhood memories, I don't relish going back even to visit the folks.

My parents are in their late eighties and early nineties with the usual litany of geriatric maladies. That's not why I don't want to go back. It has been a few years since my last visit, and I remembered how unpleasant it was. Mom never approved of my lifestyle even though that phrase isn't in her lexicon. Anyway, suffice it to say, she doesn't approve, and she's not bashful about it. Actually she's not bashful about anything. I change jobs too often, she said. I'm too interested in money. I should go to church more often, and so on and so on. "Take care of your soul, not your pocketbook," she said to me more than once.

Pop is completely different. As a man who struggled through bankruptcy during the depression, he developed a different perspective on things, especially economic things. Once as a kid I asked him for a dime to go to the movies with my best friend. "Friend?" he said mockingly. "You want to know who your friend is? I'll show you who your friend is." He thereupon pulled out the roll of bills he kept in his right front pants pocket and peeling off a dollar, pointed to the picture of the man everyone knew as the founder of our country. "Who's that?" he asked.

"George Washington," I impatiently answered.

"That's right, George Washington. He's your best friend. Don't forget that." In his early days as an immigrant to this country, the man had been hurt by relatives and friends alike, and now he trusted no one but the likes of George Washington.

Mom and pop are an unlikely couple. She is educated, he is not. He is practical, she is not. She is religious, he is not. Oh, he might have gone to church but he was always working in his store whenever there were services. Making a living was far more important to pop than going to church. After all, he had six kids to feed and clothe.

Mom came from a well-to-do family that had fallen on hard times. She felt she had married beneath her station, and she let everyone know it. When pop came to America, he couldn't read or write his own language much less that of his new country. In spite of the lack of education, he was able to amass a small fortune and return to his homeland in search of a bride. A marriage was arranged for this "successful businessman from America," even though he was from a lower class. But mom never forgave him for his humble beginnings, feeling that her brother, who was in charge of the arrangements, had been deceived, or bought off, by this well dressed "American." When he brought his bride to the New World and introduced her to the modest life that a petty shopkeeper could provide, she was distraught. No, she never forgave him or her brother.

I never understood how pop put up with it for over sixty years. He busied himself with grubbing out a living seven days a week. No time was left to worry about happiness. Making money and feeding his family was his priority.

The bus jerks to a stop in one of the chain of small towns that dot the route home. "Bingo Friday Nite 7:30," a weather-beaten sign proclaims in front of the Elks Club. Bingo, that's what awaits us at the end of a productive life. I wonder if mom or pop plays Bingo. The bus groans on.

More small towns, more bingo signs, lots of gas stations, stores with "For Rent" signs in their windows, a two lane highway lined with maple trees, and finally, I am home. The old town looks different, smaller, more run down than I remember. There is no bus station so we few travelers are dropped off unceremoniously on a street corner. I take my suitcase, disembark from the bus and begin the six-block walk to the house I used to call home. The cracked and uneven sidewalks are uncooperative as they grudgingly yield to my footfalls. I pass several vacant stores on State Street, skeletons of businesses past, grim precursors of the fate awaiting this little village. The rest are run down, victims of hard winters, too few customers, and the appetite of larger cities that inevitably sucks the life out of these small towns. Somebody gains, everybody loses.

Block by block I navigate the sidewalks and streets, Mechanic Street, State Street, School Street, and finally West Street. I'm home. What an ugly little house it is—two-story, white clapboard construction. Its architecture doesn't even have a name. It's not classic anything, not neo anything. It's just an eighty-year-old house that was slapped together by some people who needed a roof overhead.

The paint is peeling above the front porch. It needs work. Can the roof be far behind? The old man can't handle it anymore. My sister, who lives nearby, calls contractors whenever things are on their last legs. She doesn't like to do it. Pop gives her a hard time about spending his money.

I hesitate to go in, but in I must go. My footsteps are heavy on the porch but no one hears. Mom's in the kitchen in the back of the house. Pop's watching TV in the parlor with the sound turned way up. His back is to me and he doesn't hear my entrance. I pause only to drop my suitcase and walk back to the kitchen.

Mom has failed a lot since I last saw her and is surprised to see me. "You," she says. "To what do we owe this honor?" Sarcasm to the end.

"Hi Ma," I say.

"Are you hungry?" she asks. "Sit down, I'll get you something. Did you see your father? He's driving me crazy. All he does is sit in that chair, with the TV so loud they can hear it next door."

"Doesn't he have a hearing aid?" I ask, even though I know the answer.

"He did, but he lost it. He wouldn't wear it anyway. You won't believe what I'm putting up with."

"I hear you Ma. I know." It's starting already, and I haven't been home five minutes. I wonder if it can get any worse, and I know it can.

"How did you come? The bus. Aha. Why didn't you call? Your sister told me you were coming. Couldn't you tell me?"

I don't respond because to mom conversation is a one-way street. When she gets up to speed, the prudent listener doesn't even try to cross the road because the words will run him over.

"What?" she says even though I haven't said anything. Mom has a hearing aid too and won't wear it either except to watch her favorite TV programs.

"Nothing, Ma," I say in an elevated voice.

"You don't have to shout," she says. "I'm not deaf, you know."

I notice the array of prescription bottles on the kitchen counter along with little dosage cups labeled for the days of the week. The seven dwarfs are waiting patiently to go to work to cure the maladies of old age. I shake my head as I pick up each bottle to read the labels of remedies with unpronounceable names, to cure ailments I know not of.

"He won't take his medicine, you know," mom announces. "Will you talk to him? He's driving me nuts you know."

"For Christ's sake Ma, he's over ninety!" I fairly shout.

"Don't you take the Lord's name in this house!" she emphatically admonishes. "I know you're a big man with a big job and fancy everything. But when you're in my house, don't bring your atheist manners with you."

"Yeah," I mutter. It's time I said hello to the old man. I go into the living room, reach over his back and press the mute button on the remote control. Pop is a little startled.

"Hello, John!" he booms.

"How ya doin', Pop?" I ask.

"What's that?" he says.

"How are you?" I repeat slowly and deliberately. I'm not sure if he hears me or reads my lips, but he understands.

"Where's the wife? She with you?" he asks.

"No Pop, she isn't," I holler. I dutifully perform the ritual of conversing with a hearing impaired, slowly going senile, ninety-one year-old man, repeating

The Ellis House, Carthage, NY

with increased volume until some semblance of understanding is established. God, he doesn't look that old. It's too bad he can't hear well and can't find the damn hearing aid. Maybe we could talk over old times, something with meaning instead of the weather and how everybody is. We used to be able to do that in the old days. I liked to tell pop how much money I was making because I knew it pleased him. Money was an important yardstick of success to him, perhaps the only one, ever since he struggled through the Great Depression. He never understood why anybody would want to pay me the kind of salary I was earning. "Confuters?" he would say. "What the hell are confuters?"

The strain of conversation tires me quickly, and I decide to take my suitcase upstairs to find a place to sleep. My old bedroom is one of four on the second floor. It seems smaller even though the double bed has been replaced with a twin. I don't unpack because I resist any semblance of permanence that this action would imply. This way I can pretend that I'm in a room in a lower class hotel.

I sit on the bed, composing my thoughts, wondering what to do next. The room is dusty and the paint is faded. But the sheets are clean and the window shade goes up and down. What more can I ask for?

The bedroom is next to the bathroom and I remember as a kid having to listen to everybody come and go, waiting for my turn. "You're taking too long," mom would shout. Even now I know if I go in there she'll be along shortly. Her timing was always impeccable.

I hear shouts from downstairs. "Turn down that TV!" mom is saying. "What?" pop responds.

More shouting. More "What?"

I go downstairs to see if I can buffer the noise, even though I know it's useless.

"Where's your wife?" mom asks.

"She's at home," I answer. I don't want to tell her that she wouldn't come on a bet. Mom never approved of our marriage, and it wasn't forgotten.

"What's happening to this world?" she responds rhetorically. "Where did I go wrong? No manners, no respect of your elders, no church. It's no way to live, I'm telling you."

We've had this conversation before. Different time, same conversation. I glance around the kitchen and see water stains on the ceiling. "Roof been leaking?" I ask.

"This house is falling down around me," mom says. "Your father can't fix anything. Did you see what he did with the bathroom door? He wanted to cut off a little on the bottom to keep it from scraping the carpet, and he cut the top off instead! He's driving me crazy I tell you."

"So that's what happened." It didn't surprise me. Pop never was a good handyman. He neither had the time nor the training to understand the use of tools. A pick and shovel was all he had been acquainted with in his formative years. Add that to his age and you get doors chopped off at the wrong end.

"He's still a peasant," my mother says. "I don't know how much more I can take."

"Maybe he's getting even after all these years," I answer.

Mom either doesn't hear me or chooses to ignore my attempt at chiding her. "You know I don't have much longer," she announces. "If you don't make peace with God, I don't want you coming to my funeral. Not in the church anyway."

"You've got lots of time," I tell her in a lower voice. I don't like this subject even though I know she's over eighty and wearing a pacemaker, the result of a valve replacement she had eight years ago.

"What's that?" she asks.

I don't raise my voice this time and reply, "Put your hearing aid in, Ma."

"You're whispering on purpose," mom says.

"Put the goddamn hearing aid in," I shout, "or I'm not going to talk to you."

Mom struggles with whether to continue to fight with me or get the hearing aid. The hearing aid wins. She retreats to the living room where she has the prosthesis stashed. She returns shortly with a little blue box that, if I didn't know better, would think contained a diamond ring. Considering its cost, I suppose it should be classified as jewelry.

"I hate this thing," she says, fumbling with the tiny apparatus. "Your sister is the only one who knows how to adjust it."

It's always the same. Somebody else knows better than I do. That's the implication. I'm more than a little annoyed as I say, "How many moving parts does it have? How hard can it be? There's one little goddamned dial, that's all. You don't have to be a genius to adjust it." I fiddle with it. "How's that?"

"It whistles," she says as she adjusts the dial herself. "I suppose it's okay."

The small house is closing in fast so I decide to go for a walk. "Where are you going?" mom asks. "I just put the hearing aid in to talk to you."

"The hearing aid is for listening, Ma," I respond. I've got to get out before I really lose it. "I'm going for a walk."

"What do you want for supper?" she asks as I head out of the kitchen.

"Don't worry about it, Ma," I say, "I'll cook something for myself when I get back."

I took the opportunity to pop a couple of pain pills, and decided to walk down the street in the general direction of Monument Park. Maybe I can get some peace there among the headstones of a hundred fifty years ago. The ancient cemetery became a park at the turn of the last century when they ran out of room for the newly deceased. Now it's a memorial park honoring the dead of various wars.

I notice that it's well kept up, better than the rest of the town. The grass is mowed and I want to sit down but there are no benches. There used to be benches when I was a kid. They probably rotted away and were never replaced. Only the dead rest here.

I look at the obelisk with the engraved names of the fallen war heroes. I recognize many. There is representation from a cross-section of families I once knew. Small towns aren't favored by wars. They trade their best young men for medals and citations and monuments. They also give them an annual parade. What more could a dead hero ask for?

Moving on about the park, I glance at the weathered grave markers. I notice how young so many people were when they died. Parents and children buried together. I wonder what the doctors of a century and a half ago told the anxious parents. "Sorry, there's nothing more I can do. He's in God's hands." It didn't look as though God took very good care of many of those buried here. Maybe they weren't in God's hands after all or He wouldn't have let so many young, productive lives end so soon, or would He?

I'm tired and pain is wrenching my gut. I'd better head back to the old house and lie down.

When I walk in, the old man greets me again as if it's the first time today. "Where's your wife?" he asks. "Did you bring her with you?"

I don't try to explain. I just mutter, "She's home, Pop."

"Home!" he says. "Why don't you bring her with you?"

"Next time," I shout as I head to the back of the house.

Mom's still in the kitchen. I'm a little more relaxed now. The painkiller has done its job. I walk in and sit at the table where she is busy peeling potatoes.

I abruptly decide to go up to my room and close my suitcase. I don't have to worry that anyone will hear me as I trundle down the stairs and out the front door. I don't even know the bus schedule but anything would be better that this, even waiting on a street corner.

A wise philosopher once said that anticipation of death is worse than death itself.

Syracuse, NY 1999

Back to Bowling

11

LIVING IN FLORIDA, AS MANY PEOPLE correctly surmise, necessarily entails meeting a lot of seniors, i.e. old people. The elderly have acquired a number of stereotypes, all of which are based on some kernel of truth. Several of these conventional beliefs contend that seniors are impatient, penurious, cranky, talk about their health all the time, and are most interested in which restaurant offers the best early bird special. Of course you can find seniors who embody those characteristics, but I'm sure it's not only in Florida.

I actually love talking to seniors—as a writer I necessarily observe people—their appearance, their actions, and their attitudes—because there are a fund of stories lurking beneath the surface. And, I try to take every opportunity to unearth new and interesting tales.

One of the activities I went back to after I retired was the long neglected recreation of bowling. I don't like to call bowling a sport simply because anybody can do it— from eight-year-old kids to ninety-year-old grandmas. And, there is a lot of luck involved, because everyone will get a strike if they try often enough. Nonetheless, I was always a good bowler and when I returned to it, took it up seriously. Eventually, I turned pro and participated in many Senior PBA tournaments, both national and regional. It was a lot of fun and I met and competed against many of the stars in professional bowling.

It was through bowling that I met Gil Danner, the subject of my next story. Gil was an interesting guy, a WWII veteran and retired army master sergeant. I bowled on Gil's team for a couple of years and we used to stay around afterwards to have a beer and chat. Danner loved to tell stories and also had an entrepreneurial bent. He told me about a gold mine he'd invested in back in North Carolina, and how he thought starting a business franchising funnel cakes would be a big winner. All in all, he was enjoyable to talk to and I spent many an hour with him before he passed away from bone cancer.

I thought one of Danner's experiences would make good reading and the following tale is about one of his actual WWII adventures.

War's for the Birds

"DON'T YOU WORRY HONEY, I'll be back in a year's time." When he joined the Army in the summer of 1941, Gil Danner wasn't giving his girl a line. He actually believed the politicians who said his stint would only last that long and he'd be back in Boone, North Carolina the following year. Instead, three years later, he found himself slogging his way through the hedgerows of Europe, right into . . . the Battle of the Bulge.

"Damn," the reluctant soldier thought to himself as he formed up his patrol that cold December night. "I hope these goddamn rookies won't do anything stupid and get me killed." Sergeant Danner was a cook in an infantry unit and didn't look forward to being pressed into service as a foot soldier.

After two years in the Africa campaign and nearly six months of battle on the Continent, he figured he was beyond recon duty but, because his unit was shorthanded, even mess hall personnel were given field duty. Danner wasn't afraid, neither was he a reckless yahoo, just a practical man whose sole focus was to survive this "goddamned war," as he called it. And as the conflict dragged on, whenever he was slated for patrol he couldn't help but wonder if this would be when the inevitable happened.

"This damn war is chewing up people faster than they can be replaced. We're becoming an endangered species," he would say to other combat veterans. He was an old-timer at twenty-two and knew that many of these kids coming in as replacements would never get the chance to become old-timers like him. But rookies or not, patrol duty had to be pulled and it was his turn.

Danner drew up his ample, six-foot frame, spit out a stream of tobacco juice, gritted his teeth, and formed up the men in his squad of "volunteers." He paid little attention to the ubiquitous grousing and grumbling that disguised the fear the boys felt. The first thing a soldier learned to do in this man's army . . . was to complain and Danner knew and accepted that.

"Hey, Sarge, we ain't never done this before. Heck, we just got here on Tuesday," one of the rookies said.

"Never mind that crap!" Danner answered. He had to be tough because many a GI had looked at his freckled, boyish face and mistook him for a country bumpkin. "Shut up and listen up!" he barked. "We're gonna' recon a piece of this here Hürtgen Forest." He spat out Hürtgen correctly because he had learned some German from his Dutch grandparents and he not only knew how to pronounce these Teutonic names but had actually made conversation with some of the German prisoners they had taken. "The Hürtgen Forest," he continued, "is where you are, and if you don't already know it, it's damned mean territory. We've got to be extra careful out here, so follow orders and don't be makin' any unnecessary noise."

The sergeant knew that the forest, which straddled the Belgian-German border, had been turned into a bloody battleground. He saw men returning from action in those woods, and it wasn't a pretty sight. Whole regiments had been decimated, and fresh troops were continually being thrown into the dense green and white meat-grinder.

"See how thick these woods are?" he warned as they filed out of their bivouac. "These trees can kill you just as easy as shrapnel." Danner's unit had been in the forest for a month as the Allied forces tried to clear it of Germans in their push to the Rhine. He saw men impaled by splinters from overhead shell bursts. And he knew of the many perils the thicket held in its two hundred square miles of tall fir trees, deep gorges, icy streams, and swampy meadows, all of which caused it to be aptly named "Dead Man's Moor."

In more contemplative moments, Danner thought that this wouldn't be a bad place if it weren't for the war and all the damn killing. "Good hunting ground," he mused, "plenty of game, good cover and all." The squad leader often reflected on his Appalachian Mountain roots, where he had regularly stalked deer and shot birds. "But this ain't back home," he reckoned as his mind returned to the present, "and I've got to be careful how much I tell these kids, or else they'll be so goddamned scared they'll get us all killed. God, the draft boards must be scraping the bottom of the barrel. Was I ever this green?" Although in a more candid moment he knew he had been, his acquired persona no longer allowed him to admit it. The once timid, lanky, redheaded country boy didn't really know how to curse until he entered the service. Indeed, he had been just like these kids, as green as a July cornfield back in Boone. But his all-consuming concern now was for his personal safety, and when he appealed to his Captain for more experienced men for his patrol, the unsympathetic CO told him that these boys were all he was going to get, so he'd better get on with it.

The Hürtgen Forest seemed to have some order to it with row upon row of giant fir trees. Danner was told by one of the German prisoners that many of the trees had been planted at the turn of the century in honor of the kaiser, but he didn't know if it was true or not. In wintertime, the huge branches of the gigantic pines spread their wings and trapped much of the snow before it could reach the ground. Men on patrol, wherever possible, would walk as close to the tree trunks as the terrain would allow, where the snow was not as deep and navigation much easier. As Danner's squad snaked through the bright, moonlit night in single file, listening for any sounds of activity, their leader was silently thankful that it hadn't snowed in the past two days. The area was well trampled and he knew this would make it more difficult for enemy units to track them, that is, if they had the will to try.

After two hours of half-hearted probing of the forest, Danner suddenly raised his right hand signaling the men to halt. Even though they had been admonished to fan out behind him, the rookie column was following so closely that they nearly toppled like dominoes when he abruptly stopped.

Danner's ears had involuntarily perked up in a primeval response to danger. "Shh . . ." he whispered, and all of the soldiers strained to hear what he heard. There it was again, a rustling noise. Could it be another patrol off to the south? Was it friend or foe? Could it be a one of the many deer or bear that roamed the forest? Danner didn't know, so he decided to steer his squad off in the opposite direction, away from the unknown sound. "There's no sense looking for trouble with these kids," he thought. "We're only supposed to be observers anyway."

About fifteen minutes later, a sudden and barely perceptible flapping noise floated in from above, accompanied by a whooshing sound. The men, already spooked by the previous disturbance, clumsily dove into the snow, pointing their rifles haphazardly in every direction. Then they saw it. A large bird swooped down and lit on something hiding in a little gully in front of them. After a short, noisy struggle, the bird lifted off with an animal in its clutches, one nearly as big as the bird itself.

"Jesus!" one of the rookies said. "Did you see that?"

"I saw it," Danner answered. "That boys, was a big 'ole owl." He'd never seen an owl that big in the Appalachians. "Did you see the size of that mother? I've heard they'll even kill a baby deer when they're desperate for food."

The column vigilantly regained its composure and continued on its mission. They had gone about another one thousand yards or so when a fresh commotion from a different direction caused Danner to halt again. "Boys, this place is too goddamn busy for us," he whispered.

The cook had previously seen a skirmish or two on night patrol, and had even been shot at by other American troops. It was an occurrence that commanders oxymoronically called "friendly fire." He knew well the fear and panic that grips battle-fatigued men and how they could be more dangerous than the real enemy. Sergeants on patrol were empowered to use their discretion to abort missions, especially if it looked as though they might shoot at Americans instead of Germans.

"Look boys," he said in hushed tones. "Y'all have to get your asses back to camp as best as you can." After calming the ensuing fearful gasps as best he could, he whispered harshly, "That's an order!" After consulting his Lensatic compass, he traced out in the snow the routes each should take and sent them off singly at ten-minute intervals.

The sergeant waited an additional fifteen minutes after all his men had been dispatched and then he too started back to the encampment. He was happy to be rid of these kids for he knew his chances of survival were much better alone.

Danner had gone about a half-mile when he heard the crack of a shot fired from some distance behind him. "Jesus!" he exclaimed to himself after he felt the round whistle overhead. "Who the hell can that be? If it's one of those goddamned kids shooting at me, I'll kill him." Until he could determine who had fired on him, he decided to climb up the nearest pine tree to take cover. He grabbed a low hanging branch and hoisted himself up, unloosing a shower of snow in the process. Once in the tree, he could hear the patrol of men approaching, their boots making muffled, crunching noises on the packed snow. When they were near enough for him to decipher their whispered commands, he knew they were . . . Germans!

"*Sie schossen einen Geist!*" one of the enemy soldiers said. "You shot a ghost! *Es gibt niemand hier!* There's nobody here."

The Sergeant strained to listen and decipher the conversation. "We'll stop here," an older voice said. "The Americans will have to find us." Danner could barely make out the six men who had decided to park right under his tree—twenty feet below.

The boy that had been submerged inside the vigilant veteran surfaced in a flash and his heart began racing with the accompanying adrenaline rush. He began to perspire even though the temperature was near freezing. As he clung to the trunk of the tree, he forced himself to be absolutely still. The conversation below drifted up to him in hushed snatches, and Danner soon determined that the enemy patrol was mainly made up of scared young boys along with an older soldier, who betrayed some cautiousness about engaging the enemy. After they calmed down, the patrol settled in and began talking more animatedly, albeit quietly, while passing around a cigarette. The fumes curled up the trunk to the treed soldier's nostrils as he resisted the impulse to sneeze. Danner could hear the older man chastising his charges saying things like, "Be quiet. You kids are going to get me killed."

"Damn," the Sergeant thought. "More kids. I've got to be careful not to startle them. Christ, they're as scared as my boys were."

Time seemed to pass surrealistically slow for the

treed soldier as the seconds crept into minutes with the minutes hesitatingly developing into hours. Danner lost all chronological bearing as he struggled to maintain the awkward position required to sustain his refuge. The lure of sleep brought on by extreme cold had to be resisted for he knew he could easily fall victim to it. Clinging to his perch with one aching arm while the other cradled his rifle, he thought, "If these bastards don't get the hell out of here soon, I'm going to freeze to death and fall right into their laps."

Suddenly, with an awareness that was increased by his acclimation to the intense darkness, he began to sense he was not alone! "Jesus," he thought to himself, half in prayer. "There can't be someone else up in this tree!" Slowly and with some difficulty, he gripped his rifle trying to ready it for an improbable defense. He swiveled his head to the left . . . and saw nothing. Slowly he turned back in the opposite direction to stare . . . straight into a pair of large black eyes! There in the darkness, at an arm's length from the end of his nose was a huge bird . . . staring right back at him! Only the sharp fear of discovery kept him from losing his grip and falling out of his hideaway into the arms of the Germans.

The raptor that loomed in front of him was a fearsome Eagle owl, "bigger than a Thanksgiving turkey," he would later relate, with feet about the size of Danner's quite large fists. His experience with wildlife told him that these same appendages, bristling with menacing talons, could crush his arm should the bird decide to use one as a roost. And its flapping six-foot wingspan would create a wind-tunnel-like vortex that would cause snow to rain down on the Germans below. Danner didn't even want to think about the hail of bullets that would follow in his direction.

The veteran's harsh demeanor melted away as he became paralyzed with fear. He instinctively tried to communicate with the bird telepathically. "Don't you dare make a move!" he voicelessly commanded as he tried to surreptitiously position his rifle for a possible defense. The best he could do was place his right hand around the trigger housing and poke his index finger through the hole in his glove that was made for just that purpose. "There's no chance," he thought. "My hand's so cold I can't even feel the trigger." So he became reluctantly resigned to engaging the bird in a hypnotic staring match while he waited for the Germans to make their move. He no longer felt the cold as fear muted the toll the climate was taking on his body. Occasionally, when lulled into reverie by the strange serenity that settled on this improbable scene, he would think about being back in the mess hall and making a big pot of boiling soup, and how good it would taste right about now. He also drifted into reflections about how hard he had been on the younger men, and how much like the enemy camped under his tree they actually were. The only difference was that the German kids would readily kill him if they knew he was there.

Suddenly the owl made a barely perceptible motion that jarred the soldier back to his present danger. "God, I sure could use a few of my men now," he thought.

The Germans, oblivious to the drama taking place above them, went on conversing about the Americans, the war, girls waiting for them back home, and whether they would get out of the Hürtgen Forest alive. "Me too," thought Danner. "Me too."

As dawn approached, he heard the enemy leader tell his patrol that it looked like they had survived another night and they could now make their way back to their unit. They broke off their little encampment and headed east toward the German lines. Danner, as soon as he was sure they were out of range, slithered down the tree, not breaking his trance with the owl until he hit the ground. The soldier then made his way back to camp as quickly as his frozen feet would take him.

When he arrived at the encampment, a few of his men ran up shouting, "Danner's back! Danner's back! We'd about given you up, Sarge."

"Never mind about me," said Danner. "Are all my men accounted for?"

Winter Park, Fl.

12

ONE OF THE BEST THINGS ABOUT LIVING in Florida is that you can exercise out of doors all year around. When the national consciousness was awakened about the perils of high cholesterol levels, I took notice. As I usually did when approaching subjects I knew nothing about, I started reading up on this latest menace. I tried to find scientific data about how to achieve a healthful level of this fatty substance that is circulating in all our bloodstreams. What I found was that no two experts seemed to agree on the basics—what number was the ideal level, how harmful it was really, and how did one maintain the proper level. As someone trained to be a scientist, it bothers me that this debate still rages.

I believe that one of the problems with achieving and maintaining a healthful American lifestyle is the pharmaceutical industry. We have been conditioned for some time that no matter what the ailment, even if caused by profligate living, it can be ameliorated or managed with a pill. This is the result when a person's health is inextricably tied to the profits of an industry—and the drug that is supposed to save your life is practically shoved down your throat by an advertising blitz. Last week's drug is discredited as a new one promisingly takes its place. And seniors continually complain mightily about the cost of the many medications they are supposed to take. In many instances gold is actually cheaper by weight than some of these prescribed pills, ointments, or eye drops. It's a situation that has spiraled out of control, draining the bank accounts of many retirees.

As a response to my health concerns, I took up jogging. I also modified my diet significantly, cutting out sugar, caffeine, and cooking oils of all kinds. I also restricted my fat and protein intake to twenty percent of my daily caloric consumption and beefed up my complex carbohydrate consumption. The diet was extremely difficult to maintain, and the exercise wasn't always looked forward to, but it had an enormously beneficial effect on my health metrics. I jogged every day and jumped in the pool afterwards, summer and winter. My cholesterol dropped to 166, a supposedly quite healthy level, and the subsequent weight loss brought me down to high school levels. There was also a corresponding boost in energy, which resulted in my requiring less sleep. I was never healthier, even when I was a kid playing basketball. It was difficult to maintain this new lifestyle, but I kept the faith religiously for six years.

At the time I was living in a rather snobbish neighborhood in Winter Park, Florida that had a hyper-active homeowners association. Prying eyes were always spotting violations of their rules—were the lawns kept up, did you install proper shingles on your roof, etc. I was never a joiner of social organizations and abhorred the putting on of airs that I observed in that neighborhood. When you came down to it, it really wasn't so different from the countless other developments in Florida, with the exception that the homes were well above the median sales price. The number of divorces adhered to the national average, as did the gossip that followed. Perceived skullduggery or other events out of the ordinary were also greatly talked about. One of our neighbors, who drove a DeLorean automobile, was indicted for and convicted of tax evasion and sent to prison. According to the news reports, he worked for a waste disposal company that had Mafia connections and had run afoul of the law. It seems he wasn't bright enough to see that the level of income he reported couldn't possibly support his obvious lifestyle.

I had always been a do-it-yourself kind of guy and once when our fence needed repair, I bought the requisite materials and had at it. The rotted out structure was originally a wooden lath design that I had replaced once before. The problem was that the thin wood strips would rot out in a few years in the damp Florida climate. So, I decided to build a sturdier barrier made of one inch lumber. One day as I was out in the driveway busily sawing boards and building the new fence, a man drove up, got out of his car, and approached. "Are the owners at home?" he inquired. The caller was puzzled as my wife and I began laughing. "Yes, I believe they are," I responded. He was shocked to find that the owners of this house would be out building their own fence. If he only knew what else we tackled, which included painting, tiling, plumbing and electrical projects. I was quite happy to leave those environs when the time came.

I periodically met a few of my neighbors when I was out on my morning jog. One of them was a guy about whom I wrote the following story.

The Jogger

KEN LOVED TO JOG. I MEAN he *loved* to jog. I'd see him out on the road when I ran, which was every other day. I ran for health purposes only, and I hated it. I didn't hate being healthy, you understand, but having to run to achieve it always rankled me. The biggest advantage to jogging, I thought, was how good I felt on the days I didn't have to do it.

But Ken was different. He ran every day and he smiled as he ran, shouting hello to everyone on both sides of the street. You'd think he was running for office instead of his health. He'd go by me in a breeze, always with a hearty "Good morning!" He might as well have said, "Ha, ha, I beat you again!" Even the back of his head grinned as he went by.

One time I was determined to keep up with him after he passed me. I dogged his heels for a full block, and just when I was going to have to give it up, he turned the corner. I kept going straight, easing up considerably after he was out of sight.

The only other times I saw Ken was at his sumptuous neighborhood cocktail parties. Ken had an attractive wife and two handsome kids, not unlike other yuppies in the neighborhood. Elaine, his wife, looked like the consummate socialite, or at least what I imagined a socialite should look like. She was pretty in her designer frock and an extremely gracious hostess as well. At her catered parties she always kept a sharp eye on the bartenders and waiters, making sure everyone had a drink in hand, the canapé trays replenished, and dirty dishes picked up regularly. The food was always top-drawer with caviar, crab claws, shrimp, smoked salmon and a large variety of desserts. I especially liked the chocolate-covered strawberries and usually consumed more than my share. Ken and Elaine's soirees, as you might imagine, were very popular.

As a neighbor, I was always invited and usually hung out on the fringe of Ken's loud conversations. He'd be in the center of the room, that toothy grin splashed across his tanned face, a drink in one hand and a ready, bone crushing handshake in the other. He was on a first name basis with everybody. New acquaintances were quickly added to his ever-increasing list.

Ken would always regale his audiences with stories of dinners with this or that celebrity, at this or that posh restaurant. Somebody would always ask what kind of person this or that luminary was or how the food was at this or that restaurant, and Ken would always end up saying they were both swell. He made you feel he was really tight with all those famous people. The descriptions all sounded the same to me, but then I didn't know any of them and they could really all have been alike.

I never knew what Ken did for a living. Whenever asked, he would say he was in "investments." I know he didn't keep regular hours because I saw him driving in or out of the neighborhood in his bright red Ferrari at different hours of the day and night, cell phone always in hand. I figured investments must be a good business because the car was one of those European limited edition models that had to cost over $100K.

On the occasions I conversed with Ken alone, usually after he stopped me on his jog, he would deftly ease the conversation towards my personal finances—something that I was hesitant to discuss. I just didn't want to give him something else to lord over me. I did, however, get the feeling that he was zeroing in on making a sales pitch about some investment that

I needed to make. We would always agree to talk at a future date but never seemed to get around to it.

One Sunday morning, after another of Ken and Elaine's famous parties, and too many chocolate-covered strawberries, I went out for my obligatory exercise run. It was then that I heard the screaming siren of an ambulance whizzing by. I could see a small crowd gathered in the distance where it had stopped. By the time I jogged up there they had already loaded a man into the vehicle and were speeding off to the hospital. One of the bystanders said they saw a guy lying in the road and called 911 from the house across the street. They didn't know what had happened but they thought that the man had a heart attack.

The next time I saw Ken was at the funeral home. There was a large crowd of friends and neighbors gathered in the foyer. They all agreed it was awfully sad, and that Ken had seemed in the pink of health. The poor chap had a myocardial infarct while out for his daily jog. I went by the bier and gave my condolences to Elaine.

As I looked down at the corpse I couldn't help thinking that the undertaker forgot to put a smile on Ken's face.

The Ellis Family, 1963

13

ONE OF THE THINGS THAT has always annoyed me is people who feel they've cornered the market on *the truth* and further insist it is their solemn duty to convince you of their beliefs. These people go by many names—born agains, fundamentalists, evangelicals, and so on. I've always been sort of a live and let live kind of guy so, if what you believe floats your boat, good for you. Please, however, do not invade my personal space to tell me about your faith.

As a believer in science, and through much reading and cogitation, I have become a fan of Darwin's theories on the evolution of the species. To me, it doesn't make a lot of sense to believe that social man requires the threat of punishment in order to behave civilly towards his fellows. Such deterrents have been consistently shown to not appreciably modify bad behavior. It has been demonstrated time and again that it is actually in a person's best interest to make friends and treat others well because there is a better likelihood of his being treated similarly, thereby improving his chances of survival. I think that's what nature intended. However, if you wish to believe otherwise, go for it. Just don't try to convert me, please.

As you may have reasonably surmised by now, I come from a very religious family—with with brothers and sisters who became priests and nuns. My mother had numerous religious icons spread throughout the house—pictures, statues, and a smattering of prayer books and rosary beads. I was an altar boy all through school at Augustinian Academy. My parochial education not only encompassed grade and high school but college as well—a grand total of seventeen years. So you could say that I was reasonably indoctrinated in the rubrics of religion.

I've met too many priests to count, along with a number of bishops. I always had the highest regard for them, even if I disagreed with them on secular matters. However when it came to matters of faith and morals, their stated province, I objected only if I thought they weren't holding up their end of the bargain.

When our first child was born, we were living in Syracuse, and I was still in college. A problem arose because we wanted to get our daughter baptized, and we didn't belong to any parish. We went to Sunday mass at the college or any of several churches in the area. But with our finances being what they were, I didn't want to join a parish and assume the financial obligations that come with that commitment. Now, however, our little family was forcing my hand.

I called a parish that was nearest to the college and spoke to a priest there. "I'd like to join the parish," I said. "Where do you live?" he asked. I told him our address and he looked it up in his parish directory. "Hmm," he said. "Well you're outside our boundary but I think we can make an exception." "Great," I said as I gave him our information. Before we concluded, I mentioned that we had a newborn for which we'd like to schedule a baptism. "What?" he shouted. "You want to join our parish just to get your child baptized? No sir, you're out of our jurisdiction," he said and he hung up on me.

Wow, was I surprised. We were in his boundary until I mentioned the baptism. Wasn't bringing another member into the Church important? What could this man of God have been thinking? We ended going back home to Carthage to get our little one baptized.

Years later, when we moved to the Pittsburgh area, my wife and I thought it would be nice if we enrolled our children in parochial school. Our previous location didn't have any near us so our children went to public schools. Down to our new parish school went my wife with the four youngest who were of grade school age, and when the principal saw the gaggle of new faces, she became visibly alarmed. "We are terribly overcrowded," she said. "You'd be better advised to take them to the public school." I was somewhat upset at the news because I had been brought up in a climate where parents were told they had a sacred duty to give their children a Catholic education by sending them to parochial schools.

Nonetheless, our eldest daughter chose to attend a Catholic high school in the area, but her brothers and sisters went on to public school, and never experienced the joys of a parochial school environment.

That wasn't the end of our difficulties at this particular parish. There was a young assistant stationed there, a priest who encouraged youth participation in the conduct of the mass. Our son Chris joined the group and was soon singing solos during mass, some of which brought tears to the eyes of the congregants. I got to know this young priest fairly well and could sense the frustration he was having with his old school pastor, a man who didn't like this modernism at all. He also didn't like the idea of having these kids on the altar during the mass. "It was unseemly," he said and banned the group from the sanctuary.

A group of us parents whose children were in the youth group, and who wanted to resolve the impasse, scheduled a meeting with the pastor. All we heard was a number of hackneyed platitudes he had memorized as a seminarian and had never updated. I was disgusted, to put it mildly, and decided to protest by organizing a financial boycott of the church. "We have to hit them where it hurts," I said, "in the pocketbook."

What a firestorm that created! A group of us would stand out in front of the church handing out leaflets to parishioners, while enduring the insults of the other Christians going in to mass. "Commies," they shouted. "Go someplace else, if you don't like it here!" This was a real eye opener for me. We had tried to open the discussion to allow the kids to keep singing songs from the altar, to no avail. We wanted to let others know the situation and to solicit support. However, there was a significant group of conservatives in the parish who also didn't like having the kids in the sanctuary.

The situation caused a stir in the Pittsburgh Dioceses and a select group of us were invited to meet with the bishop. I was appointed spokesperson for the group. The bishop, who was also of the conservative school, was none too happy with what was going on. During the course of the meeting, I happened to mention that he had some other problems under his jurisdiction as well. Some of his nuns were teaching things that were heretical in nature, and I gave an example. Our daughter had brought home some of her parochial school teachings, one of which concerned a nun claiming that natural disasters were God's way of taking care of problems such as overpopulation. I mentioned that this was but one such heresy that had been debunked by the Church more than once.

The bishop, who had made it eminently clear that he was backing his pastor, began sputtering and loudly called me out, "Do you believe in divine providence, my son?" I smiled and replied, "Well, bishop, if you define it for me, I'll tell you whether I believe in or not." Jaws of the clergy gathered around the table suddenly hit the table and the bishop was rendered speechless. I think it was then and there that I crossed the Rubicon with the Pittsburgh dioceses.

The meeting ended and the final verdict was the status quo. The young assistant priest left his vocation and married one of young ladies of the parish. We also left that parish and became nomadic and sporadic churchgoers in the Pittsburgh dioceses.

In my mind this was not what should have happened. I had thought that Vatican II was supposed to encourage more Church membership, not drive people away. I felt that these old men had become so systematized they had lost sight of the purpose of their vocations. These experiences, among others, caused me to look at men of the cloth in a more critical light.

As mentioned before, I enjoy meeting and talking to members of the senior set and it so happened that just such a chance encounter led to the following tale about what actually happened to me one Sunday morning at a local discount store.

Getting Religion at K-Mart

As I hurried past the Salvation Army kettle on my way into K-Mart, I affected all the hard-earned assurance of a self-made man, which I was. A terse, "I gave at the office," was my brusque rejoinder to the bell ringer stationed at the front door. I had developed a lack of patience for do-gooders, especially those connected with religion, and had come to view the holiday season with condescension because of all the begging that goes on. My money had been made the hard way, and I wasn't giving it to just anybody who asked.

I love shopping at K-Mart, and any of the many other discount stores I've frequented, even though I had long ago acquired the means to shop wherever I wanted. Ever the avid bargain hunter, I cruise the aisles with ease, and "Attention K-Mart shoppers!" is still music to my ears. I can spot a blue light special from five aisles away.

I knew where everything was and I quickly found the oil filter I needed and hustled over to the express checkout counter. I was going to change the oil in my Lexus and wanted to get it done before lunch.

"It's a good thing we're not in a hurry," I said, with a tinge of sarcasm, to the elderly man just behind me in the slow-moving line. A young, and obviously inexperienced cashier, a lad in his early twenties, no doubt doing his stint as a management trainee, seemed to be the cause of our delay.

"Well you've got a lot more time than I have," responded the old man with the salt and pepper crew-cut and matching mustache.

"Why is that?" said I, my curiosity piqued. Truth be known, I liked conversing with older men because I hadn't taken advantage of the opportunity with my father, a fact I'd regretted ever since the old man died last year. So now I not only readily accepted opportunities to discourse with senior citizens, but actually initiated conversation with them, as I did today. Maybe it was a desire to find men who could act as surrogates for my father.

"Because you're much younger than I am," the elderly gentleman replied.

"You don't look that old to me," I said, having myself gotten to the age where one is flattered to think he doesn't look as old as he really is.

"I'm eighty-three!" the man exclaimed proudly as he leaned slightly on his cane, a prosthesis that seemed to be the only concession to old age he was willing to make.

"I don't believe it," I said as I took a closer look. And in truth, the man didn't look a day over sixty-five . . . at least not to me.

"I'll prove it," the frisky gentleman said as he reached into his back pocket and dragged out a fat, tri-fold wallet that old men seem partial to. The bulging billfold's compartments were securely held intact by a large rubber band.

"OK, OK," said I. "Anybody who guards his wallet like that isn't about to lie. You don't have to prove it." But the old man was insistent. He stretched and pulled the rubber band until the chubby wallet a miniature file cabinet of the man's historical records. The billfold

Salvation Army bell ringer

housed an abundance of cards, IDs, and various association memberships, past and present. I couldn't help but think, "this is the American Express guy who never leaves home without it."

Out came the driver's license. "See," the old man pointed with pride. "I was born in 1926." The picture on the card verified that Joseph Albert Metz was indeed eighty-three years old.

"Well, Joseph," I remarked, "you certainly don't look eighty-three. You're in pretty good shape for your age." And I meant it. Although thirty years the man's junior, I couldn't help but wonder if I would look as good when, and if, I reached that ripe old age.

Old Joseph was eager to continue the conversation, seemingly flattered by the attention I was giving him. "I've seen it all," he went on. "Yep, I've traveled all over the world, seen it all. I've seen heaven and I've seen hell, and it's all right here on earth," he said. "Do you believe that?"

Hell on earth was something that I could identify with, and I began to feel a strange kinship with this discount store philosopher. "I can't argue with that," I said.

Just then a large, younger chap with a premature paunch immediately behind Joseph interjected with, "What do you mean by that?"

Turning towards the interloper, Joseph responded emphatically, "Just what I said." I could see the old man was not shy despite his short stature and advanced age. "Heaven and hell are here, right on this earth," he repeated even more forcefully.

"Don't you believe in the bible?" asked the intruder, leaning forward with his chin jutting out, a bit like a schoolyard bully spoiling for a fight.

I suddenly became irritated. Not only had this fellow interrupted my pleasant conversation with old Joseph but had also broken one of my unwritten rules—invoking the bible. That not only aroused my ire but also gave birth to a bad taste in my mouth.

Joseph however, with the look of a journeyman who had been down this road many times, dismissed the question. "I know what I'm talking about," was his abrupt reply.

"Don't you believe in God?" the intruder continued. "I happen to be a minister, and if you read the bible, you'll see that you are speaking heresy."

I became even more agitated and decided to take a closer look at the meddler. To me the man seemed more like a roustabout than a minister. His jeans and checkered flannel shirt were soiled with more than one day's labor. His face, dour for a man of about thirty, sported a black, sad looking mustache that draped around the corners of his mouth. Out from under the bill of the Jesus emblazoned baseball cap, two dark, intense eyes punctuated his plump face.

"So this is a minister," I thought. "I wonder if he preaches off the back of a pick-up truck." Actually, I'd had a lot of experience with clergymen, and over the years became disenchanted with the hypocrisy that many espoused. This man looked to be a prime candidate to reinforce that predisposition.

"Look," Joseph replied, "I was a minister myself, and I know all about the bible." Another card energetically fetched from his mini file cabinet ostensibly proved this. "If I tell you that heaven and hell are here on earth, you'd better believe it." With that he turned back to me and I, of course, cheerfully supplied a measure of assent, even though I wasn't overjoyed that I was now confronted by two men of the cloth. "Well, at least they're quarreling among themselves," I chuckled to myself.

The younger man was not easily dissuaded from dispensing his brand of brimstone and continued with revivalist missionary zeal. "That's heresy," he repeated. "You should know better."

Old Joseph was undeterred. "Let me tell you something young fella, I used to teach in divinity school and I never saw the likes of you there." Another card fetched from the chubby billfold was produced for verification. "And furthermore, you don't know what you're talking about."

"You must not have taught the bible," the self-proclaimed minister retorted.

"I taught all the bible had to offer and believe me, what I'm telling you is the truth."

"I don't believe you could have been a minister," the young man challenged. "You're going to hell and you won't see the light until the day after you die, and then it'll be too late."

"Listen to this guy," old Joseph said in a somewhat amused voice, turning back to me. "He's telling me I'm going to hell. What kind of minister do you think he is anyway? Look at the way he's dressed. Who'd have him as a minister?"

"He's obviously a judgmental one," was my reply, admittedly one that fairly dripped with sarcasm but did not do justice to the depth of my displeasure. I had quickly decided that not only didn't I like the look of this preacher but also severely doubted his clerical claim. "And besides, what's he doing shopping in K-Mart on Sunday morning?" I added.

The more I thought about it the more agitated I

became. "Where do you get off telling him or anybody else they are going to hell?" I demanded.

The argumentative evangelist was undaunted that he now had another heretic in his sights. "You're no different," he said. "You're going to hell too!" There it was, sentence had been pronounced on me as well!

The anger that had been fermenting in my darker depths since the confrontation began suddenly flared up in an incandescent display. Involuntarily, my body coiled up like a snake ready to strike, and my face felt as though it had been splashed with battery acid. I was shocked as my speech became slightly slurred, and anyone standing nearby might have assumed that I had suffered a minor stroke. I had to resist the urge to reach over Joseph and grab our antagonist by the throat.

"You're a . . . jackass!" I sputtered to the seedy evangelist, not caring or noticing that everyone within earshot was staring at us.

The debate had gone well beyond the level of discount store propriety, as low as that standard might be, and the cashier began to show visible signs of discomfort. He refused to make eye contact with me, or any of the combatants, choosing instead to look down at the merchandise set before him, checking and rechecking the prices. K-Mart's training had obviously not prepared him for such encounters.

"You don't scare me," the mugging minister shot back at me.

"You're too stupid a jackass to be scared!" I bellowed.

Old Joseph, although visibly surprised, seemed delighted by my spirited defense. He reached out his hand and gave me a vigorous handshake. "I'm glad you agree with me," he said.

Ugly indignation, however, wouldn't let go of me

and I continued sputtering and shooting nasty stares at the so-called minister. Temporarily bereft of my usual articulation, I suddenly realized that I couldn't have recited my ABCs clearly, even if my life depended on it.

The clerk, swaying and jiggling from side to side, finally finished ringing up my simple purchase. He smiled thinly as he accepted my money and gave back change.

The old man, grinning with vindication, bid me a cheery good-bye as I marched out of the store.

In the short walk to the exit, my sanity began to return along with a burning sensation in my cheeks. I couldn't decide if I was angry or just totally embarrassed.

The emaciated-looking Salvation Army bell ringer accosted me a second time. "Won't you give a little something for the needy?" he asked.

I paused for a moment and looked more benignly at the supplicant. I found myself fumbling with my wallet and then quickly pulled out a twenty-dollar bill and dropped it in the pot. "Jesus loves you," said the Salvation Army.

14

OCCASIONALLY, AFTER I RETIRED, I WOULD GET calls from acquaintances who were still active in the consulting game. They needed a resume that might impress their clientele, and thought mine would fit the bill. Initially, I was happy to accept these offers, largely because my consulting experience had become a dim and dark memory. I thought these assignments might actually be intellectually stimulating, and a nice change of pace.

It didn't take long for me to remember what I had tucked away in the further reaches of my memory. Companies generally hire consultants for one of two reasons: either to oppose an opponent's views or to support their own. They like nothing more than to brandish a report by experts as proof positive of their positions. As a result, it becomes a delicate proposition to render a verdict that is hostile to the views of the person who hired you.

From a consultant's perspective, he wants to provide an opinion that will favorably dispose the client to give him follow-on work. After all, this is how he makes his living and getting contract extensions for follow-on work is one of the preferred ways of getting additional business.

So, consulting work becomes a delicate act—balancing the interests of the client and those of the consultant. As a result, I did only a few of these jobs and went back to writing as a more enjoyable avocation.

One of my consulting buddies was a guy I've known for many years. Mike used to call on me at the university as a sales rep for the computer company I eventually went to work for. I gave him a really hard time, as I did all sales representatives. He once got so discouraged that I had to take him aside and tell him there was nothing personal involved, that it was just business. He ended up actually going to bat for us with his company whenever we had a dispute. We've remained friends over the years.

Mike had a dynamic personality, very upbeat and positive, and eager to climb the ladder of success. He didn't talk much about his past, and I didn't get many opportunities to quiz him. Once when we were out on a job together, I got him to loosen up and chat about his childhood, failed marriage, his dad, and his military experience. I was inspired to write the following story about Mike's experiences as he related them to me.

We Kill for a Living

"I WAS JUST AN EIGHTEEN-YEAR-OLD KID," Mike said, "fresh out of high-school when I joined the Marine Corps."

We were sitting by the motel pool drinking beer—just a pair of consultants, away from home, relaxing, enjoying the camaraderie of conversation that passes between business associates after a long day at the office. As we sat in our lounge chairs after a refreshing dip, I found myself staring at the prominent scars on Mike's right leg. He noticed where my eyes had landed, and I reddened slightly, feeling like a peeping tom caught in the act. The incident would trigger one of those all too rare moments when friends let their guard down and begin to talk about things—things they would normally be loath to remember, much less discuss. I never suspected that my rather innocent glance would prompt Mike to take a trip aboard the memory train to places he hadn't visited in a long, long time—his days as a young Marine in Vietnam.

With his eyes narrowing slightly, Mike kept on. "My Dad had been a Marine, a decorated WWII veteran of the invasion of Iwo Jima—one of the fiercest battles of that war." The words unemotionally cascaded out as Mike brushed lightly over his broken home, getting in trouble at school, weighing a mere 150 pounds, not being very tall, and trying to figure out what he should do with his life. There was a war on and the draft was looming. The idea that he should escape to Canada never crossed his mind. Perhaps joining up with the toughest branch of service would let him escape his problems. "Dad had always said you had to be a man to be in the Marines, so I guess I wanted to prove that I could be a man too."

Mike hadn't told his father he was joining and when Dad found out he shook his head and gave his son but one piece of advice. "Don't ever tell them your old man was in the Corps because they'll pick on you unmercifully." Mike admitted he was puzzled and didn't understand why this was but made a note to keep that fact a secret.

"Mom wasn't too happy," he continued, "but off to boot camp I went—to Parris Island with its swamps and snakes and the never ending marches and bivouacs." It was easy to form a mental image of this scenario because hardly anyone hasn't heard, or seen in movies, how recruits are quickly introduced to the shock of Marine Corps training—complete with drill instructors' in-your-face insults and harangues. Mike admitted it was a rude awakening for him as well, as he sardonically added, "You don't have to be a sadist to be a DI, but it doesn't hurt either."

What seemed to stick most in his memory was the double time drills where all the recruits were exhorted to shout, "Kill, kill, kill!" at the top of their lungs, while running down the company street, making his scalp tingle and the blood rush through his veins. The DIs' mission was to continually remind their charges who they were and why they were there. "We're Marines— and you will become lean, mean, killing machines!" they were told—over and over until they all, at one time or another, proudly invoked the mantra, "We kill for a living!"

"I don't know why it is," Mike continued, "whether it's homesickness, or fear of what you're getting into, or what, I don't know, but boot camp is where you make some pretty good friends. I bonded with a guy named Larry from New York State, up near the Canadian border. We started looking out for each other. He'd have my back and I'd watch his." As Mike recounted it, Larry was a tall, shy boy with dark hair, more athletic than he, and a high school dropout. But these differences didn't seem to matter—sort of an affirmation of the old adage that opposites attract. They paired up on the rifle range and in all of the many teamwork drills they were put through. "If we had to kill for a living, Larry and I were going to do it together," he added with a wry smile.

When basic training finally ended, Mike was surprised and pleased that his dad showed up at Quantico for his graduation ceremony. His old man cut an impressive figure, all decked out in his Master Sergeant's uniform—standing tall and straight, complete with the obligatory brush cut. Everyone took notice of all the ribbons, battle stars and oak leaf clusters on his chest, especially the drill instructors, who were very, very impressed. Mike's face betrayed how proud he was of his father that day, probably prouder than he'd ever been, if he would dare admit it. Father and son basked in each other's admiration as Dad told Mike how happy he was that his son was following his career path and had become a man in the same branch of service that he had joined some thirty years before.

But the drill instructors were not happy that young Mikey hadn't told them about his decorated father when they had originally asked, especially since the base commander had invited his Dad to sit with him on the reviewing stand. "They took me aside and gave me a couple of not too friendly farewell pokes for keeping that a secret," he chuckled. The DIs had asked, and as his Dad had advised, he didn't tell. The Marines were really sore that they had missed the opportunity to initiate Mike into the Corps in the traditional way.

"You can't believe the relief you get at completing basic training," Mikey continued, "and for not quitting, as many tried to do." However, after a week's leave to visit his mom back in North Carolina, the reality that he would soon be sent off to war set in.

"Let's say my mom wasn't tickled that I was going off to Vietnam," he offhandedly added. Left unsaid was that following in his father's footsteps, knowing where that trail had ended for her, only compounded her unhappiness. "It was then that mom quit calling me Mikey," he remembered. "I was just Mike to her after that." Although he had tried his best to assuage her fears by claiming that the Marines had prepared him well for the task at hand, she remained apprehensive. Of course, he neglected to mention that they killed for a living. But she already knew that.

Next came the long train ride to San Diego to await further orders. Mike felt compelled to mention, a bit sheepishly, that celebrating the end of basic training wouldn't be complete for a newly minted Marine without a ritualistic visit to Tijuana, Mexico's whorehouses, which he and Larry dutifully did, albeit with some trepidation. "We had to let off steam and when the pimps down there tried to take advantage of us, we warned them to be careful because 'we kill for a living!'"

But the respite from the rigors their killer roles demanded was short lived, and after just a week, Mike's unit shipped out for Vietnam.

A week after arriving in 'Nam, both young men found themselves perched atop a numbered hill that strategists back at headquarters felt had to be held at any cost. "We were replacements for guys that had been wounded or killed, and it didn't take us long to realize that any one of us could be next. It was then I first began to wonder what I'd gotten myself into," Mike related rather pensively.

Any rational person can understand how being surrounded by fear and death would administer a shock to a young man's system. Thoughts they might have had, that their life expectancy stretched out in a long straight line over the horizon, would be called into doubt when they came face to face with the death that surrounded them. Mike and his buddies, all of whom had successfully made the arduous passage from kids to killers, soon realized that this war business was a two-way street. They hadn't given much thought to the notion that the other side also harbored guys who killed for a living.

The swagger in their step slowly seeped out like air escaping from a punctured tire on one of their Jeeps. Coping would soon take the place of sauntering, and the ways they coped were many and varied. "I was shocked when I first saw guys smoking dope," he said. "A bunch of grunts would be sitting in the jungle casually passing around joints." Both Mike and Larry began to wonder what the hell they were doing there, especially when they realized that nobody up the chain of command seemed to care.

"We shared a two-man tent along with all our gear—backpacks, helmets, flak jackets, rifles, grenades, ammunition, and extra clips. We were warned that ole VC Charlie wouldn't give us much notice when he decided he was going to retake Hill 37." The real estate they were perched upon had been bought and paid for with the blood of several comrades, and they had to be ready at a moment's notice to repel any counterattack. "We slept in our clothes with our boots nearby, waiting to hear somebody holler, 'Gooks on the wire!' We were supposed to grab our rifles and run out, and start shooting in the direction of the perimeter. It sure kept us on edge."

Now immersed deep into the story, Mike hesitantly recalled the night he and Larry were given an order to man the checkpoint at 2200 hours. At the appointed time they slipped into their boots, grabbed their rifles and headed out. "When we arrived at our post we were shocked to see that nobody else was there—we were all alone. Larry whispered to me, 'Where the hell is everybody?'" Mike didn't know, but he suddenly realized that in the excitement and anticipation of their first real combat, they'd not only forgotten to lace up their boots but didn't have their flak jackets on either.

"I'll run back and get them," Mike said as he scurried off. He was in the process of strapping on his body armor when he arrived back at the post. He hadn't even had time to pass Larry his jacket when he heard the swoosh of an incoming mortar round. It landed close enough to knock both men off their feet. Mike regained consciousness to a stabbing pain in his right thigh. He also felt a burning sensation on his face and when he touched it, he had to suppress a scream. "Blood was dripping down my chin onto my flak jacket," he recalled as his face gave an involuntary twitch. "And my jacket was pockmarked with shrapnel."

How long it had taken to regain his senses he didn't know, but the first thing he thought to do was check on Larry who was lying on the barren ground nearby. "I leaned over and asked if he was okay. He looked up at me, and with what seemed like the last bit of air in his lungs, he whispered, 'Mikey.' Even in the dim light I could see Larry's torso had been laid open by the blast. I didn't know if the Cong had breached the perimeter, but I screamed for a medic anyway." When Mike reached down to touch his throbbing leg with his hand, his palm came up dripping with blood, and thoughts that he might bleed to death put him in a panic. "Medic, medic!" he hollered again. The pain that showed in his face in the telling might have matched the pain he was feeling back then.

Mike doesn't really know how long he lay there before he heard someone whispering to him. It was a stocky, muscular guy with a Red Cross armband, dragging a low-slung cart, called a "mule," behind him. "OK," he whispered, "I've got you." Although overcome with relief, Mike couldn't move.

"Get on the mule," the medic said.

"I can't!"

"Get on or I'm going to have to leave you and go get someone else!"

"I can't," Mike repeated and now readily admits that he was sobbing—from pain or fear he's not certain—as he struggled to get up.

"Alright," the medic said. "Grab the side and hold on. I'll drag you and the mule." And with a mighty effort, Mike managed to get a grip on the cart's rail as the medic heroically dragged him and the mule up the hill to comparative safety.

"Wait," Mike said. "What about my buddy?" "I can only take one at a time," the medic replied. "You just hold on."

The wounded Marine remembers being surrounded by some men in his unit who were shouting, "Hang in there, Mikey. Semper Fi! Semper Fi!"

"Where was everybody at the checkpoint?" Mike weakly asked. "Didn't you get the word? It was called off," was the reply.

"Can you believe that?" Mike said in a sad voice that was rimmed with more than a tinge of disgust. "It had been called off, and nobody told us."

A medic administered a couple of shots of morphine as Mike was loaded on a stretcher and hauled over to the helipad. He was passing in and out of consciousness

U.S. Marines, Vietnam

but remembers hearing the whomp, whomp, whomp of a helicopter and soon felt himself being loaded and strapped into the medivac, along with one other stretcher. When the light of the breaking dawn and the continual jostling motion of the helicopter helped Mike regain his senses, he craned his head to take in his surroundings. His eyes caught sight of a toe-tag on the body bag next to him. There was just enough light for him to make out the name. . . Pvt. Lawrence. . . It was Larry!

When the chopper landed in Danang, Mike remembers that his tears were still flowing, and he could feel them leaking into his ears. He was rushed into a field hospital where OR personnel took large scissors and cut away all his clothing and then sprayed him down with a torrent of water. The next thing he remembered was waking up in a hospital bed, with his face, arms, and legs swathed in bandages. When able to be transported, he was taken to Japan for further rest and healing.

After a long recuperation period and some R&R, he was sent to Okinawa, which was the primary staging area for Vietnam deployment. Mike had been ordered back to combat, even though his wounds weren't completely healed—the one on his right thigh continued to ooze a tan colored pus. But, there were manpower shortages and quotas to be met, and beleaguered commanders demanded more troops.

"I was looking out on the ocean and remember thinking, 'this is the end for me.'" He plunged into depression, fearing that his fate was to end up just like his buddy Larry. "But I was lucky," he sighed. "I was reexamined by a doctor who was willing to buck the brass. He pronounced me unfit for duty, and I was finally sent home to a Navy hospital in Philadelphia and later discharged."

The rest of the story I pretty much knew. Mike went to college on the GI Bill, and after a series of marketing jobs, ended up on a consulting team. Although the scars are ugly and the anguish is real, Mike is a changed man from those Marine Corps days. He no longer talks about killing for a living. He also refuses to visit the Vietnam Memorial—not even to gaze upon that dark, stark wall. . . to make out Larry's name one last time.

Ghosts of the Past

15

A LL THE PRECEDING CHAPTERS in this book could be considered a disinterment of my past, an exhumation and examination of the many ghosts in my closet. There are similar specters in just about everyone's past if only they would take the time to dredge them up. Writing has been a therapeutic way for me to disinter mine.

As I write, I am mindful that the memory plays tricks on just about everyone—me included. But the stories told here are as fresh in my mind as if they occurred yesterday. This is no doubt due to the fact that I've told them orally to many people over the years, without variation or noticeable embellishment. The reader will have to take my word for this, I know, but I feel secure that the foregoing, minus the changes I mentioned in the Foreword, along with a few dramatizations, are quite true renditions of actual events.

I will close this narrative with a whimsical story I wrote that epitomizes the many dreams I've had over the years when reflecting on the past. I sincerely hope you've enjoyed this trip through my looking glass.

I Don't Believe in Ghosts

I DON'T BELIEVE IN GHOSTS. Why not? Because I've never seen one. Well, not until last night, that is.

I was on my way home when I heard a distant clock tolling the hour. The full moon that had been making its way across the eastern sky suddenly seemed to dim. At that moment, I saw a shadow pass across its face. It was the image of a dark robed figure riding a small but mysterious contrivance that made no noise as it arced across the sky. "I must be imagining things," I said to myself as I peered into the horizon. It was then I saw dozens of bat-like creatures following the robed rider and the eerie scene sent shivers down my spine.

Then I heard it. A high-pitched cackle . . . or was it a scream? I couldn't tell but the pace of my footsteps involuntarily increased along with my heartbeat. My breathing was coming faster as I reached the walk leading up to the front door of my home. The moon had suddenly gone completely dark . . . or had it just slipped behind a cloud?

I stumbled up the steps to the front porch, landing on my knees and hurriedly tried to retrieve the house key from my jacket pocket, but it was trapped in the folds. The more I struggled to get at it the more entangled it became. In desperation, I tried to turn the handle of the door but the unresponsive knob told me it was locked. I saw an unnatural light creeping over the threshold but couldn't tell where it was coming from, or why it would be there. Then I heard that cackle again . . . or was it a scream? I was about to scream myself when I suddenly sat bolt upright. My head was spinning. Where was I?

I looked at the closed door and saw that eerie light filtering into my bedroom from under the threshold.

Still woozy, I slowly got out of bed and stumbled to the door and this time it opened on the first try. I mopped my brow with my pajama sleeve as I wobbled out into the family room. There I saw my wife watching TV. It was a rerun of the Wizard of OZ.

"Why honey, you look as if you've seen a ghost!" she exclaimed.

"Me?" I said. "Naw, I don't believe in ghosts."

ACKNOWLEDGEMENTS

OVER THE LAST THREE YEARS, SINCE THE publication of my first book, *Kisses from a Distance*, I have made many friends who have read and/or encouraged my writing. Several readers of *Kisses* made a point to tell me, not only how much they enjoyed the book, but how they were also anxiously awaiting the sequel. I told them all that I had no intention of mounting a sequel effort, and that I didn't consider what came later to be all that interesting. I kept those thoughts in mind, however, as I tackled other projects and have to admit that this book was greatly influenced by the encouragement of those readers.

This particular work evolved over several years and was only recently considered suitable as a memoir. I had originally thought of seeking a publisher for only the short stories contained herein (and actually found a reputable one willing to take on the project), but the realization that that genre is one of the more difficult to market gave me pause. I finally came up with the idea that morphed into *Dam Foolishness*.

Chris Ellis, a talented songwriter and performer, did all the graphics for the book including the cover design. I was always impressed with the way Chris introduced his songs with a narrative about how he came to write it. It gave the songs a special feel, so I decided to borrow that idea to create a preamble to each of my short stories. I think it gives them more meaning and I hope everyone enjoyed that approach.

I also must thank the people who read first drafts of the manuscript and offered encouragement. Howard Splete, a Carthage boy whose dad was my high school basketball coach, was always ready to read anything I wrote and offer his comments and encouragement. Bob Tiernan, a fellow LeMoyne alum, and another boy who passed through Carthage in his youth, prevailed on his partner Julie Wells to go over the final draft with a fine-toothed comb. She picked up too many errors and suggested corrections to mention. For this effort I am truly grateful. I must also thank my friend and fellow author, Charles Malouf Samaha, who also contributed mightily with proof reading this work.

I should also mention Sisters of Saint Joseph archivist, Sister Mary Gregory; Sister Norma Bryant; and Shannon Margery for providing several of the pictures used in this book. Also, thanks go to the Town of Wilna Archives, Jefferson County, New York for the old pictures of Carthage.

I must also give special thanks to Scott C. Davis, owner and publisher of Cune Press, for his continued faith in my writing ability and for his willingness to step out of his normal genre to produce this work. I also must mention Billy Mitchell and Hien Nguyen, editors who toil for Cune, for their diligent efforts on my behalf.

Raff Ellis, a former computer industry executive, resides in central Florida. He is the author of the award-winning literary memoir *Kisses from a Distance.*